LOST IN AMERICA

HOW YOU AND YOUR CHURCH CAN IMPACT THE WORLD NEXT DOOR

BY TOM CLEGG AND WARREN BIRD

Loveland, Colorado

LOST IN AMERICA:
HOW YOU AND YOUR CHURCH CAN IMPACT THE WORLD NEXT DOOR
Copyright © 2001 Thomas T. Clegg and Warren Bird

Visit our Web site: **www.grouppublishing.com**

CREDITS
Acquisitions Editor: John J. Fanella
Editor: Brad Lewis
Senior Editor: Dave Thornton
Chief Creative Officer: Joani Schultz
Art Director and Designer: Jean Bruns
Computer Graphic Artist: Joyce Douglas
Illustrators: Jean Bruns, © Lisa Henderling/SIS (pp. 13, 65, 108)
Cover Art Director: Jeff A. Storm
Cover Designer: Wirestone
Cover Illustrator: Nip Rogers
Production Manager: DeAnne Trujillo

Unless otherwise noted, Scripture taken from the HOLY BIBLE, NEW INTERNATIONAL VERSION®. Copyright © 1973, 1978, 1984 by International Bible Society. Used by permission of Zondervan Publishing House. All rights reserved.

LIBRARY OF CONGRESS CATALOGING-IN-PUBLICATION DATA
Clegg, Tom (Thomas T.)
    Lost in America : how you and your church can impact the world next door / by Tom Clegg and Warren Bird.
        p. cm.
    Includes bibliographical references and index.
    ISBN 0-7644-2257-X (alk. paper)
    1. Evangelistic work--United States. 2. Christianity and culture--United States. I. Bird, Warren. II. Title.

BV3790 .C567 2001
266'.00973--dc21   00-067189

10 9 8 7 6 5 4 3 2 1   10 09 08 07 06 05 04 03 02 01

Printed in the United States of America.

TABLE OF CONTENTS

SECTION ONE: CHANGES

SECTION TWO: CHOICES

SECTION THREE: CHALLENGES

■ The message of the gospel never changes. But American culture does. *Lost in America* will help you identify fresh ways to relate the timeless message of Christ to searching people in your life today. Both individual Christians and local churches will find this book useful.

Franklin Graham
CEO, Billy Graham Evangelistic Association

■ We need more pragmatic leadership material to fortify our development as leaders. This is one of the top books I've read in a long time. The ideas are well supported with experience and data. All innovative-minded leaders should have this book in their libraries.

Doug Murren
Director, Square One Ministries

■ Tom Clegg and Warren Bird do not believe that the American church can do what it has always done and achieve different results. They recognize that the new millennium requires a totally different view of evangelism. In *Lost in America* they have produced the freshest, most insightful, and practical witnessing tool we've seen—a must-read for every Christian and every pastor.

Eddie and Alice Smith
President and Executive Director,
U.S. Prayer Track

■ *Lost in America* is a book that has a powerful and helpful message for every pastor in our nation—and beyond. The authors do a great job of not only identifying the challenges faced by the church in America, but also graphically presenting some practical, biblical solutions for building the authentic, loving relationships needed to share the good news of Jesus Christ with our neighbors and friends.

Paul Cedar
Chairman, Mission America

■ What a refreshing book! Tom Clegg and Warren Bird have pumped new excitement into evangelism by showing that every Christian can reach out through personal relationships to bring others to Christ. The authors demonstrate that our programs of evangelism are no longer effective, and we are using yesterday's tools and yesterday's ideas to reach people in today's world. In the final analysis, they tell us to "go get them personally."

Elmer Towns
Dean, School of Religion, Liberty University

■ With a convincingly upbeat approach, *Lost in America* is the freshest book I've seen to inspire you to initiate evangelistic efforts. The illustrations sparkle. Every time I picked it up, I felt like I'd had another shot of sparkling water. Open it up and drink deeply.

Carl George
Director, Leadership for Ministry

■ A fast-moving book filled with practical ideas and gripping illustrations to help the church reach the lost. The message of this book hits home.

Robert E. Coleman
Director of the School of World Missions and Evangelism, Trinity Evangelical Divinity School

■ This book debunks—sometimes shockingly—the spiritual complacency and distorted self-perception of American Christianity. Hopefully, it will move you, as it does me, to a sobering re-evaluation and perhaps recommitment to a lifestyle that is sacrificial, obedient, and mission-minded.

Sam Metcalf
President, Church Resource Ministries

■ In a compelling fashion, Tom Clegg and Warren Bird diagnose the spiritual state of our nation. Rather than ending on the depressing note of the marginalization of the church and the secularization of our culture, they proceed to offer an inspiring blueprint for being Great Commission Christians in our own communities. The book will be particularly helpful for small-group discussion and training events. I'm looking forward to a journey through the book with our church leadership team!

Jonathan Schaeffer
Senior Pastor, Grace C&MA Church, Cleveland, Ohio

■ God calls all of us to be "world Christians," living for the fulfillment of the Great Commission worldwide. We can start reaching out immediately, right where we live, as the Spirit gives us missionary eyes for the world next door. Clegg and Bird set forth a pathway for congregational outreach in an eminently readable, liberatingly insightful, and motivationally practical way. I don't know of a church anywhere that wouldn't greatly benefit from this powerful book.

David Bryant
Founder and President, Concerts of Prayer International

■ If you want to remain complacent, don't pick up this book. If you want God to transform you, read *Lost in America* and prayerfully reflect on your situation. Then follow the prompting of the Holy Spirit. You will experience a deeper relationship with God as you intentionally build relationships with those who do not yet have a faith relationship with Christ.

Bob Logan
Executive Director, CoachNet, Inc.

■ If you desire to reach your full potential in sharing the good news with your relatives, friends, and neighbors, read *Lost in America*'s uncompromising, unsettling, and unconventional message. You'll be glad you did.

John C. Maxwell
Founder, The INJOY Group

■ Cleverly written and compellingly argued, *Lost in America* shatters our complacency and challenges us to do whatever it takes to reach the growing numbers of lost people in one of the greatest mission fields in the world: the USA. We owe it to ourselves—and to our friends and neighbors—to read and heed this powerful book.

Mark Mittelberg
Evangelism Champion for the Willow Creek Association, and author of Building a Contagious Church

ACKNOWLEDGMENTS

T his book would not have come together without Jodi Clegg's un-
tiring and undaunted research efforts, frequent trips to the library,
endless Internet surfing, careful manuscript preparation, eagle-
eyed proofreading, and fearless truthtelling. For all this, Tom once
again admits that he married way out of his league. Warren agrees.

We'd also like to thank a number of friends who gave their valuable
time to review early manuscript drafts and make insightful suggestions.
Their combined efforts made this book much stronger than we could
have crafted alone. Readers included Matt Aberhasky, Arden Adamson,
Randall Bach, Gretchen Bird, Michelle Bird, Nathan Bird, Ames Broen,
Steve and Sherrie Brown, Jerry Burnamen, Phil Claycomb, Pat Colgan,
Tom Collins, Roger Cutler, Robert Damon, Merton Dibble, Bill Easum,
Jock Ficken, Sam Fritz, Dennis Gorton, Stephanie Hall, Wayne Harris, Jim
Hobby, Dave Hudson, Dale Hutchcraft, Kep and Debbie James, Tom
Johnston, Mike and Kimberly Kopp, Gene Kucharsky, Lisa Lakatos, John
LaRue, Paul Leavenworth, Chuck Loftis, Bob Logan, Mike and Pam Lum-
bard, Dave and Cheryl Lyle, Reggie McNeal, Tim Mercaldo, David Miller,
Phil Newell, Steve Ogne, Stan Ott, Dan Reinhardt, Martin Sanders, Larry
Segelken, Bud and Muriel Smythe, Len Sweet, John Vawter, Gail Vosler,
Terry Walling, Craig White, Diane Lahlum Wido, and Ron Willoughby.

Warren adds his special thanks for the friendship, evangelistic passion, and mentoring from Dale Galloway, Michael Slaughter, Bob Cush-
man, and Carl George. Tom extends his thanks to Bob Logan, Steve
Ogne, Sam Metcalf, and the Church Resource Ministries family; to his
accountability partners Greg Schwab and Ed Carlson; to his prayer partners and ministry supporters; to the Open Bible Standard Churches who
stand with him in ministry; and most of all to Chelsea and Lindsey Clegg
for their loving and patient support.

We also appreciate the careful, creative, and risk-taking team we
worked most closely with at Group Publishing: Thom and Joani Schultz,
Dave Thornton, John Fanella, Jeff Storm, Pam Klein, and Kerri Loesche.
And a special thanks to the insights and expertise of our editor, Brad Lewis.

Finally, Tom and Warren want to thank the hundreds of caring
friends who made up the mosaic of God's love that finally got through
to each of us.

INTRODUCTION
WE ARE DIFFERENT

"Trees move the wind." So said the gods of science, technology, and human ability.

Today the winds have shifted. Today people are more open than ever before to the idea that the most powerful forces in this world are invisible and spiritual. In days past, that God was unseen was often given as a reason not to believe in God. Today being unseen is all the more reason to trust. Maybe the wind moves the trees.[1]

We're thrilled to live in an era of incredible openness to spiritual conversations among friends. People today are open to God—and to many different gods. If people could verbalize their experiences, they might

Our goal is to help you visualize what God does through other-directed compassion, friendship, and love. This is the heart of evangelism at its best.

describe the journey something like this: "I haven't yet accepted the Jesus you tell me about; but if I do, it's because I've seen him in you." Wow! The Holy Spirit can help us cultivate those see-God-in-me relationships. "For it is God who works in you to will and to act according to his good purpose" (Philippians 2:13).

We're fans of the Christian who described his job here on earth as being prepared for heaven when God brings him home and taking with him as many people as possible. God can use *you* to do just that in your life as well.

Our goal in *Lost in America* is to help you visualize what God does through something so simple and basic as genuine, intentional, other-directed compassion, friendship, and love. This is the heart of evangelism at its best. Our perspectives will challenge prevailing stereotypes, change misdirected efforts, and lead to more joyful results. Success will not be measured in the amount of shipping cartons (what we print) or in new information (what you learn), but in lives transformed through God's handiwork.

ONE BIBLE, ONE MISSION

Law	Mandate: "All peoples on earth will be blessed through you" (Genesis 12:3).
Poetry	Music: "Declare his glory among the nations" (Psalm 96:3).
Prophets	Moral obligation: "Help the poor and needy" (Ezekiel 16:49).
Gospels	Message: "Make disciples of all nations" (Matthew 28:19).
Acts	Method: "[They] preached the Word wherever they went" (Acts 8:4).
Paul's letters	Mentoring: "Follow my example, as I follow the example of Christ" (1 Corinthians 11:1).
Other letters	Models: "Whoever claims to live in him must walk as Jesus did" (1 John 2:6).
Revelation	Motivation: "With your blood you purchased men for God from every tribe and language and people and nation" (Revelation 5:9).

Every church as a mission outpost.

Every pastor as a mission mobilizer.

Every believer as a missionary.[2]

TOM CLEGG WRITES:

It was painful for me not to stay in Africa. My missionary appointment there had reached its end, and I was going back home. I couldn't wait to see loved ones, but I really wasn't happy about going back to the United States.

Please don't misunderstand; I love the United States, and I'm patriotic to a fault. I was going back to "one nation under God"—the land colonized by religious groups, where its charter documents repeatedly reference God, where both houses of Congress open in prayer, and the only country in the world that puts "in God we trust" on its currency. It's a place where social observers continue to note that "religious affiliation is by far the most common associational membership."[3]

Not one of my African friends could claim that kind of national heritage.

I was certain that God had called me to him in May of my senior year of high school, when I gave my life unreservedly to the Lord Jesus Christ—and from that day on, I have never regretted the decision. Years later, as I was leaving Africa, I had become just as certain that my vocation in life was to be a missionary of the gospel.

Yet I was convinced that my homeland wasn't a mission field. After all, there was a church building on practically every corner and every kind of Christian ministry you could think of in almost every city. What was I supposed to do?

Where I had served in Africa, the gospel was vibrant and powerful. It produced changed lives, healthier communities, and vibrantly alive churches. In North America, the gospel has the same inherent power, but somehow it has become so misdirected, misrepresented, marginalized, and disobeyed that the saving message of the love of God through the cross of Christ has become strangely irrelevant to people's lives.

When I speak in U.S. or Canadian churches about doing evangelism in Africa, people look at me with wonder, amazement, and curiosity. When I talk to them about doing evangelism here, their eyes glaze over and their interest disappears.

As I made my journey home, my heart burned within me. I felt lost and disconnected. It was the loneliest time of my life. Not yet married, I bounced from church to church and relationship to relationship all the while trying to find out what was wrong with me. I reasoned, "The problem has to be me. Somehow I must have missed God's direction, misread his leading, or missed him entirely." I wanted to go back to my missionary life, but circumstances prohibited it. If I had to stay here, then why couldn't I serve God here as I had in Africa?

Then, during a worship service one morning at my home church, it struck me: I *could* do exactly that. I'd been so busy asking God questions, and all the while his call to me had not changed. I was pleading, "Why can't I go back?"; God seemed to be pleading, "Why can't you stay?"

That conscious decision transformed my entire outlook. I realized that only my location had changed. The calling and assignment had not.

> I was pleading, "Why can't I go back?" God seemed to be pleading, "Why can't you stay?"

Within weeks I met a young woman named Jodi whom I eventually married. She forced me to talk through these issues. About that time, a church in Illinois contacted me, wanting to harness my passion for overseas missions in their local ministry.

After moving, getting married, and re-entering local church ministry, my sense of mission began to return. Our home became a place of refuge for young people. An unwed mother came to live with us, and at our kitchen table, she made the decision to keep her baby. Neighbors became friends, they attended church with us, and many of them decided to follow Christ.

Lay leaders found their own calling through groups we led in our home. Soon I found a love for my community and country I thought I'd lost forever. I found it not in something new, but in something that had never left.

In a matter of years, I was leading initiatives to plant new churches all across our country, just as we'd done in Africa, and helping to develop innovative strategies designed to touch lives for Jesus Christ in every segment of our society. Without realizing it, I'd become a missionary again. Today, my family and I serve North America through the mission agency, Church Resource Ministries, based in Anaheim, California.

Through *Lost in America* I hope to show you how a change in perspective can result in a changed heart and changed behavior. Welcome to *my* mission field! I pray that I can help you along on the same journey as you come to view your neighborhood, your school, your workplace, and even your church as *your* mission for Christ.

> *Lost in America* **shows how a change of perspective can result in a changed heart and changed behavior.**

WARREN BIRD WRITES:

While we were vacationing in England, my family took a walking tour of one of the oldest sections of London. "This place has a curious history," our guide explained as he pointed to a refurbished building containing upscale apartments. "Centuries ago, French Huguenot immigrants to this area built that structure as a church building. When they moved on, Jewish people populated this area, and the building became a synagogue. The neighborhood changed again, and the structure became a Buddhist temple. Today it's a different kind of temple—one where urban professionals go inside and count their money."

As we walked to the next spot on our tour, my wife, teenagers, and I were amazed at how the neighborhood had changed so much over the centuries—and how the God we worship didn't seem to be part of that community anymore.

We saw that same thing happen when we lived in Chicago. We were part of an innovative church that was strongly committed to reaching out into the community. Twenty years and three pastors later, that church doesn't exist, and the building where we met is now owned and used by the Islamic Education Center.

These experiences made me think about what my legacy will be when my wife and I eventually leave our neighborhood in Suffern, New York, which is just outside of New York City. What lasting mark will I leave of the presence of God?

It's encouraging to dream of what might happen if a movement of God occurred in my area, a part of what many would say is the most influential metropolitan city in the world. Suppose that all of my neighbors—or even just half of them—could experience the life-changing gospel and became real followers of Jesus Christ? The ripple effect could be worldwide!

What lasting mark will I leave of the presence of God?

I care deeply about my neighbors and friends in this community, and I tell myself that I'd do anything imaginable to help them come to a close relationship with God through Jesus Christ. Recently my wife, Michelle, who leads a women's Bible study in a nearby home, took several of the members to a rally where someone explained very clearly how to find peace with God. Two of the women asked if they could pray to receive Jesus Christ into their lives.

That same week, I took several men of the neighborhood to a breakfast meeting where we talked about starting a Bible discussion group. All said yes, and we started the group. Through our meetings, these men have taken God seriously at a level they've never before experienced.

Why couldn't that kind of breakthrough happen in your neighborhood, too? My heart's passion is that you could feel what could happen if we all helped one another become more other-oriented. Imagine what might happen if every follower of Jesus and every church moved more intentionally in the direction of helping people become whole through Jesus Christ.

Unless everyone who claims the name Christian becomes what that name implies, then our churches, neighborhoods, and society will have no hope of spiritual survival. Yet God is willing today, as in the past, to transform "me first" people into the servants of the world.

For the first time in North American history, people in a large segment of the population are growing up without being influenced by Christianity in any way. What a time to make a difference!

A *Newsweek* poll finds that two-thirds of Christian adults say it's important that non-Christians convert to Christianity.[4] My prayer is

People today are growing up without being influenced by Christianity in any way. What a time to make a difference!

that you will join with us in feeling compelled to become more personally involved in this challenge.

Both Warren and Tom write:

Although we've both contributed equally to this book, for clarity, we've chosen to let Tom's voice be the predominant one in the upcoming chapters.

As you continue to read, please know that we've prayed for you. We've asked God to use this book to help Christians look with

We have asked God to use this book to help Christians look with fresh eyes at the outward focus their local church needs to pursue.

fresh eyes at the outward focus their local church needs to pursue. We want God to work through us to reach *our* neighbors for Christ—and we have earnestly prayed that the same work of God will happen in *you and your church.*

Thanks for becoming better acquainted with us. Now we want you to become better acquainted with what's happening in *your* world and community. Before you continue reading, would you pause to sincerely ask God to use you, as the following prayer suggests?

Dear Lord of all life, I acknowledge my own brokenness and constant need for the purifying power of Jesus Christ. I lay all my personal inadequacies before you and pray for your wisdom, knowledge, understanding, and courage.

• As I read these pages, I ask for a transformational faith that takes bold risks for you.

• Fill me with a compelling concern for the eternal well-being of my friends and neighbors.

• Use my imagination to dream of creative, contemporary, relevant ways to point people to the wonders of the salvation Jesus offers.

• Show me how I can honor you through the gifts you've given me.

• Please bring friends alongside me who can be stretched with me so that together we can spur one another ahead in love and good deeds.

In Jesus' name, amen.

SECTION ONE

CHANGES

CHAPTER 1

CHURCH IS DIFFERENT

Churches are going out of business because they refuse to change. Any church that doesn't shift from "ministry as status quo" to "ministry as mission outpost" will die or become hopelessly irrelevant.

BIG IDEA

Monday, April 13, 1970, dawned as a quiet day in the news. None of the news stories had any particular sense of urgency—a small plane had crashed in Iowa, the anti-war movement continued to grow, John and Yoko's marriage was being blamed for the breakup of the Beatles, the Senators had beaten the Red Sox 6-5, the Brewers had swept a doubleheader with the White Sox 5-2, 16-2, and Apollo 13 was on its way to the moon.[1]

This ho-hum day suddenly received a powerful jolt at 10:07 p.m. (EST). The Apollo 13 flight, two days, seven hours, and fifty-four minutes into an otherwise routine mission, experienced a terrible mishap. Moments later, from a distance of 203,980 miles, the now immortal words of astronaut Jack Swigert crossed the void of space and crackled over the speakers at Mission Control: "OK, Houston, we've had a problem here." In disbelief, or at the possibility that they'd misheard, the controllers radioed back, "This is Houston. Say again please." Jim Lovell then spoke, confirming the worst: "Houston, we've had a problem."[2]

Apollo 13's five-word message galvanized NASA into action and arrested the attention of an otherwise distracted public, as was so dramatically portrayed in Ron Howard's film *Apollo 13*. By that time, NASA had become so good at launching flawless missions to the moon that the country had stopped paying attention. Now the world came to full alert as everyone realized that the spacecraft had malfunctioned and that three astronauts had become pilgrims in peril in the deep void of space.

The next day, both the House and Senate passed resolutions calling on the American people to pray. At St. Peter's Square, the pope led

50,000 people in prayer for the safe return of the astronauts. In New York City, thousands of people gathered to read the news headlines and to pray in Times Square. Walter Cronkite summarized everyone's concern, "Perhaps never in human history has the entire world been united by such a global drama." [3]

As the world watched and prayed, NASA raced to find a solution. Engineers soon realized that there was only enough power to get the astronauts part of the way home. Flight Director Gene Kranz refused to accept that outcome as an option. In Howard's film version of the story, Kranz said, "I want you all to forget the flight plan. From this moment on, we are improvising a new mission." His goal was totally clear: "We've never lost an American in space. We're...not going to lose one on my watch!" His strategy was equally plain: "Failure is not an option!" When a NASA official remarked, "This could be the worst disaster NASA's ever experienced," Kranz disagreed. "With all due respect, sir, I believe this is going to be our finest hour," he replied. [4]

Working with unprecedented determination and focus, NASA did the impossible. It rescued the astronauts from certain death in outer space and did indeed achieve its finest hour.

"HOUSTON, THE REST OF US HAVE A PROBLEM TOO"

The words "Houston, we've had a problem" may have arrested the world's attention back in 1970, but something has broken today that is even more life-threatening. It has been malfunctioning in my life and in countless churches across North America, and most of us are just now hearing the wake-up call.

The way Christians do church today is the equivalent of ignoring millions of desperate, but unrecognized, cries for help. We're letting an increasing number of our neighbors and friends die without a personal exposure to the life-giving good news of Jesus Christ. Unless we make some drastic changes, many people are likely to perish, and we'll fail in the mission of what God has called us to become and to do. This world is damned and doomed to a devil's hell, and in the final analysis, our behavior indicates that we really don't care.

> The way we do church today is the equivalent of ignoring millions of desperate, but unrecognized, cries for help.

THINK ABOUT THIS AS YOU GO TO SLEEP TONIGHT

Before you wake up tomorrow, thousands of lives will be changed forever. In a typical day in the United States...

• 10,799 babies will be born and 6,403 people will die. There will be 6,148 marriages and 3,110 divorces.

• 3,246 women will have an abortion and 3,445 unmarried women will give birth to a child.

• 84 people will commit suicide, 45 people with the AIDS virus will die, and 43 people will die from alcohol-related car crashes.

• 4,630 fifteen-year-old girls will have sexual intercourse for the first time, 1,312 students will drop out of high school, and more than 6,000 people under the age of 18 will try their first cigarette.

• 28,206 people will be arrested, 4,274 of them for drug abuse violations.

• 3,396 households will declare bankruptcy, and 63,288 people will receive food stamps.[5]

In that same 24-hour period, thousands of people will reach spiritual turning points:

• 411 Americans will convert to the Muslim faith, 872 will become Mormons, and more than 5,000 Americans will either join a church or receive Christian baptism.

• 8 churches in the United States will close their doors for the last time, and 6 new churches will be started.[6]

Most important, within the next 24 hours, by our best estimates, several thousand people in the United States will die without knowing Jesus Christ and will spend an eternity separate from him as a result.

What will you do to give eternal hope to someone before another day goes by? It can begin as soon as you take the prayerful initiative to talk with a friend about your relationship with God.

Lost in America dreams that your church's finest hour lies ahead. It's a dream about making other people a priority; about living the gospel and being Jesus to your relatives, neighbors, and friends; and about being a relevant witness through relationships. Ultimately it's a story about how God can work through people like you and me, and through churches like yours and mine.

"HOUSTON, I HAVE A PROBLEM"

I recognized that something was wrong with me after I led my first board meeting as pastor. Under my leadership, we languished through wasted hours of meaningless bickering over the most nonessential stuff imaginable.

The high point of our discussion had to do with keeping people from using the church building. Someone had spilled sugar in the fellowship hall. One of the board members was upset about it and wanted to pass new, restrictive rules.

I remember going back to my apartment, lying on my bed, and calling out to God, "Please don't let me be like them!" It seemed as if church was a hobby for most of the people on the board. They had no life in the community. They had no connection with the people our church said it was in business to serve. Instead, their big issues seemed to be power and possessiveness. I told God, "I don't want to be part of a church where we focus on what I just led us through. I didn't say yes to ministry because I wanted this."

I couldn't sense any answer from God. I concluded that I had to be in another place or in another role before God could really use me.

In the coming weeks, I proved convincingly that I didn't know how to help the church transition back to its original call and first love—fostering contagious, life-transforming, faith-filled relationships with Jesus Christ. I'm sure I frustrated the church as much as I frustrated myself. I continued to find that my ministry as a pastor was far removed from all the things that had made me want to go into full-time Christian service in the first place.

Weeks later the phone rang, and the director of a missions agency asked, "We're starting a new project in Africa. Would you consider being a part of it?" After praying about it, I said yes and resigned from the church. Once I got to Africa, I felt I was able to "walk my talk" as a Christian. It was delightfully refreshing.

In Africa I also discovered that the things that limited my effectiveness didn't revolve around a change of geography.

> My real problem was as close as my head—I had an inadequate perspective.

My real problem was as close as my head—I had an inadequate perspective. The issues were all inside of me.

When I returned to the United States, I had a lot more hope for the church, but I still didn't know how to help. I caught myself in the same nonproductive pattern, as if everything that had happened in Africa meant nothing.

I particularly remember one weekend. I was married and lived in Virginia at the time. I had been up late that Saturday night—out with my wife Jodi. When the alarm went off early Sunday morning, I had a hard time responding.

As I rushed out the door of our little condo to attend the before-church prayer meeting, I saw my neighbor Tyrone sitting in his pickup truck, looking distraught. When he noticed I was looking his way, he quickly turned away so I wouldn't catch his gaze.

I glanced at him again, then once more as I put my key in the ignition. This time he was looking back at me. For a reason that might be best explained as an action of the Holy Spirit, I couldn't get the key to turn.

I got out of the car and called over to him, "Are you OK?"

He rolled down the window and said, "Terrie wouldn't let me in the house last night."

I didn't know what to do. I had to get to church. I had important responsibilities that morning. Yet here was something that I sensed to be another God-given responsibility. Would I be like the religious man in Jesus' story of the good Samaritan and turn away when someone seemed to be in need of compassion and mercy?

Jodi and I had been working hard to build a meaningful friendship with this couple. I knew that if he and I talked, it wouldn't be just a hit-and-run case of caring. It also wouldn't be the first time Jodi or I had needed to make a choice of whether to stop, listen, and care for our neighbors or go to another church activity. This kind of choice seemed to be something that God regularly asked us to make.

I walked over to Tyrone's truck and got in. As I listened to him, I stole glances at my watch. Prayer meeting time came and went. A while later, Jodi and our daughter came out of the house and saw me. I waved, and Jodi gave me a curious but somewhat understanding look and waved in return. She drove to church, leaving my car still parked in the driveway. Tyrone and I talked through the church hour, and we were still at it when Jodi came home.

Quick-thinking people had covered for me at church, but others were upset. "Why weren't you here?" many asked by phone that afternoon and in person at our evening church service.

I answered with great joy, "I was leading my neighbor to a faith relationship in Jesus Christ." That really didn't matter to most of them.

As I processed most of the responses, something became profoundly clear to me: I was supporting a system where reaching out largely drew criticism. I wanted to change the culture of our church so that we would rejoice when someone found peace in God and became new through Jesus Christ and so that an opportunity to be a good Samaritan would be viewed as the right choice to make.

> The people I thought I was in business to reach were the last ones I was spending time with.

At first I wanted to draw a line in the sand and blame the church.

As I prayed and talked with friends, however, I realized that if any line were to be drawn, it would be an arrow that pointed to me. I was guilty in terms of how my time and energy were spent. The people I thought I was in business to reach were the last ones I was spending time with. I hadn't aligned my life with the things God was teaching my mind and heart.

Over time, my wife and I kept making the choice to intentionally reach out to these and other neighbors. Doing so required a dramatic change in our priorities. This couple began coming to church with us and bombarded us with questions about God.

One day, Terrie sat down at our kitchen table and asked Jodi to tell her all about Jesus. The last time we were in contact with Terrie and Tyrone, their marriage was stronger than ever, and they were

This book is about sorting through the attitudes behind your talk and walk as a representative of Jesus Christ.

actively involved in a church. Our experience with them has been a benchmark for our lives to this day, helping us constantly re-evaluate our commitment to lost people.

These lifestyle changes came, but only with great difficulty. The reaction at church bothered me deeply, but I had so much baggage that I didn't know how to respond in a positive way. What God has taught me since then has freed me to place a priority on intentional relationships with people who don't yet know Christ. As I've shared these insights over the years in conference settings, others have found help too.

Those discoveries illustrate what this book is all about: sorting through the attitudes behind your talk *and* walk as a representative of Jesus Christ. As you experience breakthroughs and victories in this area, you'll be able to help others in your church to do likewise.

Your life can take on the clarity of a space expedition or a rescue mission—you can be focused, determined, stretched, and challenged.

UP CLOSE & PERSONAL

Downtown Houston Had a Problem Too

In 1839, when the population of Houston was only 2,000 and Texas was an independent republic, a missionary to Texas organized what is known today as First United Methodist Church of Houston. Over the next century, the congregation grew, as did the city.

In the 1980s with the fallout from the oil crisis, the inner city began to deteriorate. Crime increased and retail merchants moved to the suburbs en masse. Church attendance also plummeted. A survey printed in the local papers revealed that more than 50 percent of the people of Houston would not be willing to go downtown for any reason.

The situation became critical by the late 1980s. Bill Hinson, the pastor of First Methodist, met with the previous pastor. "Can First Church endure as a viable congregation if the present trend continues?" he asked. His predecessor, a much-loved mentor and friend, couldn't imagine a breakthrough. "Even God Almighty can't keep that congregation for fifteen more years," he replied.

Instead of giving up, Hinson pointed the congregation back to its original missionary vision. He preached a series of sermons entitled Our Church: A Monument or a Mission Station in the Twenty-First Century. He led the congregation to seek God and to reach out to Houston's many newcomers.

In an amazing turnaround, the gray-haired, declining congregation has become one congregation with two campuses—the original downtown location plus a new campus on the fast-growing west side of town. The same pastoral staff ministers at both locations. Both campuses are growing and attracting young families.

Because of the church's commitment to reach out to the lost, many people are finding hope in Jesus Christ. "We have more opportunities to win people for Christ with a dual campus than we could ever have enjoyed at our downtown campus alone," says Hinson.

WHAT DOES OUR "MISSION CONTROL" TELL US?

The essence of any church is its mission. The essence of God's mission is extravagant love, which Jesus Christ communicated and displayed for us on the cross. "But God demonstrates his own love for us in this: While we were still sinners, Christ died for us" (Romans 5:8). The essence of God's love, as he showed us, is unilaterally choosing to trust across immense, incredible barriers—to make a difference, by God's power, in the lives of other people, for now and for eternity.

The essence of God's love is to make a difference, by God's power, in the lives of other people, for now and for eternity.

Every church's relationship with God and among its members must always include the invitation for others to join in. Jesus makes a strong statement in the parable of the great banquet: "Go out to the roads and country lanes and make them come in, so that my house will be full"

(Luke 14:23). And 1 John 1:3 affirms, "We proclaim to you what we have seen and heard, so that you also may have fellowship with us. And our fellowship is with the Father and with his Son, Jesus Christ."

Too often, churches lose sight of what they're all about. Instead, we focus primarily on our own fellowship and become terribly insular and inbred. As Bill Easum says, "Church members…who see their church as the focus of their mission have missed the entire point of Christianity."[7]

> **Your church—beginning with you—must change its heart and its behavior, learning to build intentional relationships with people who aren't yet Christians.**

The choice is simple. Your church—beginning with you—must change its heart and its behavior, learning to build intentional relationships with people in your community who aren't yet Christians. The alternative is what almost happened to First Methodist Church of Houston—fading away as an increasingly irrelevant, declining congregation.

RENT THIS MOVIE

The Truman Show
(Drama/Comedy, PG)

Truman Burbank is an insurance agent who lives in the Florida community of Seahaven. One day as he goes to work, a klieg light falls magically from the sky. This curious event helps him finally discover what the rest of the world already knows: that he is a prisoner on the world's biggest soundstage; that his wife, friends, and relatives are all actors paid to interact with him; and that his life has been broadcast for years as the world's most popular television program.

What to look for: Think about Truman's world before he discovered that he was out of sync with reality. What parallels can you draw between Truman and a church that has become hopelessly irrelevant to the lost? What made Truman want to leave his world and engage with "real" people? What should the motivation be for a church to do likewise?

CONNECTIONS

North America—Leader of Christianity?

Answer each question, guessing if necessary.

1. What country has the Christian church with the largest attendance in the world? _____

2. What is the dominant religion in that country? _____

_____

3. What's the location of the world's second-largest Christian church? _____

4. What is the dominant religion there? _____

5. In what country do you think the world's largest Buddhist temple is located? _____

6. Where is the world's largest Muslim training center? _____

_____

7. What country has the world's largest Jewish population? _____

_____

8. Which country has the world's eighth largest Hindu population?

_____

9. Where is the world's largest training center for Transcendental Meditation? _____

10. In the United States, what ethnic group is most responsive to the gospel? _____

1. Korea

2. Buddhism

3. Lagos, Nigeria

4. Islam (although Christianity is a close second)

5. USA (Boulder, Colo.)

6. USA (New York City)

7. USA[8]

8. USA. The ranking is as follows: India, 815 million Hindus; Nepal, 21 million;

Bangladesh, 15 million; Indonesia, 4 million; Sri Lanka, 2.7 million; Pakistan, 2 million; Malaysia, 1 million; and the United States, 0.8 million.[9]

9. USA (Fairfield, Iowa)

10. Asian-Americans. While 5 percent of U.S. Asians were believers in 1991, 27 percent currently accept Christ as Savior—a 440 percent increase.[10]

Discussion Questions

1. Many people feel uncomfortable when they hear that things aren't so good here in America. Why do you think that's so? Would you rather someone told you the truth about a difficult situation or just told you something to make you feel better about the situation?

2. If you had a chance to send a radio message to heaven from earth, what would you say? Would it be, "Heaven, we have a problem"? What exactly *is* our problem?

3. What would you suggest if heaven radioed back, "What do you want us to do for you?"

4. Do you believe the problem we have can be solved? Why or why not?

5. Imagine if someone were to secretly watch your day-to-day life. Would the observer conclude that you're part of the problem or part of the solution? Why?

CHAPTER 2

ARE FUTURIST TRENDS DIFFERENT

Here are seven eye-opening reasons to challenge patterns of business as usual in your church and mine.

BIG IDEA

n the movie *Back to the Future*, Dr. Emmett Brown, a wild-haired, bug-eyed scientist, was in big trouble. On a crumbling ledge of the clock tower fifty feet above the ground, he was desperately trying to join two electrical cords together. If it didn't happen in the next few seconds, his friend, Marty McFly, would be stuck in 1955.

One of the two cords was attached to a lightning rod where, at precisely 10:04 p.m., a bolt of lightning would strike. The other cord ran to an exposed wire stretched above the adjoining street.

Everything depended on Doc's being able to connect the two cords in time. With the thunderbolt's supercharge from the skies, Marty could use the converted sports car to get back to the future.

> "In many parts of America we have become the kind of place to which civilized countries used to send missionaries"—*William Bennett*

Doc Brown faced a host of obstacles, from crumbling concrete to falling trees. All tried to thwart his attempt to connect Marty with the future. Meanwhile the curious police officers stood by and watched.

In his book, *Culture Shift,* David Henderson uses this scene from the movie to make the point that a similar situation takes place when a pastor steps behind a pulpit or a neighbor talks about spiritual matters with a spiritually seeking friend: "God has spoken. Words of life-inventing grace and world-transforming power spill out into human history like a bolt from heaven." [1]

The vitally needed bridge between worlds contains life-changing potential. And we are too distracted to notice as the Spirit streaks by, much as the police officers in *Back to the Future* totally missed the significance of what was happening in front of their eyes.

CLOSE&PERSONAL

Building an Outreach Momentum, Despite the Obstacles

The church in the quaint New England town could offer lots of reasons why it shouldn't reach out. Its lovely chapel-like worship area was filled to capacity. What more could anyone expect for this one hundred-year-old landlocked congregation with tremendous challenges both for meeting space and parking?

Instead, Calvary Evangelical Free Church in Trumbull, Connecticut, hasn't allowed any challenges to stand in the way of its outreach commitment. "There are so many people who are lost, and so many creative ways to reach them," summarizes Dave McIntyre, the senior pastor since 1985.

The church has a strong heritage as a beacon of light in its community and around the world. "The former pastor of thirty-seven years was a man of tremendous evangelistic passion, both locally and for foreign missions," says McIntyre. "Because of him we have a culture of strong interest in evangelism."

As strong as that legacy is, it continues only through one-on-one interactions. "The door that has always been the most effective is the personal invitation," McIntyre says. "It happens whenever God's people are excited about what God is doing in their lives."

As God transforms individual lives, the church invites participation through attractive programming—everything from strong children's ministry to seasonal drama done with quality and excellence. Slowly but surely, new people find connection points, even though, as McIntyre notes, "we've made as many mistakes as we've made wise choices."

In order to make room for more people, the church leadership shifted two of the three Sunday morning worship services from the beautiful sanctuary to an attractive but plain gymnasium. They've also been very creative with parking issues. And they've encouraged as many ministries as possible to include an evangelistic dimension. At one point, when the church staff created a list of existing lay-run outreach efforts, it took a multiple-page brochure to describe all of them.

"Church is all about recognizing gifts, and setting people free to use those gifts," says McIntyre. "Our job is to consistently seek God and be faithful. God's job is to give the harvest."

How dare we assume that *your* church, with you as a part of it, is headed for the same kind of who-cares-if-we're-stuck-in-yesteryear trouble? Your church *might* be the exception; but consider the seven startling statistics in the following pages that show the kind of society we've become. As William Bennett notes, "Despite our wonders and greatness, we are a society that has experienced so much social regression, so much decadence, in so short a period of time, that in many parts of America we have become the kind of place to which civilized countries used to send missionaries." [2]

As your review the statistics that follow, notice the silver lining to our problem. The church in North America is missing an incredible opportunity that exists only a few steps outside of its front doors and sometimes even *inside* its front doors. The unchurched population in the United States is so extensive that, if it were a nation, it would be the fifth most populated nation on the planet after China, the former Soviet Union, India, and Brazil. Thus our unchurched population is the largest mission field in the English-speaking world and the fifth largest globally. [3]

> The unchurched population of the United States is the largest mission field in the English-speaking world and the fifth largest globally.

Neither the United States nor Canada is a land of practicing Christians. We have nearly two hundred million reasons—people outside an active relationship with any church—to confirm that statement. [4]

THE SEVEN DEADLY STATISTICS

The Western world is the only major segment of the world's population in which Christianity is not growing. [5] The following sobering information shows why your church must become a lighthouse of hope to people around you who need Christ.

FACT #1: *The percentage of adults in the United States who attend church is decreasing.*

U.S. churches are growing, but not enough to keep pace with the population. [6] Of the nearly 280 million people in the United States today, [7] only 40 percent of the adults said they went to church last week. That's down from 42 percent in 1995 and quite a slide from 49 percent in 1991. [8] Other research indicates that only about half as many people *actually go to* church as *say* they do. [9]

According to researcher George Barna, the number of unchurched adults is increasing. One in three U.S. adults (33 percent) is unchurched, which translates to 65 to 70 million people. (People were classified as unchurched if they had not attended a Christian church service during the past six months other than a special event such as a wedding, funeral, or holiday service.)[10] George Hunter, a leading authority on the church's impact and effectiveness, says the situation is far worse: "In America, there are 120 to 140 million functionally secular people, many of whom are nominal members of our churches."[11]

> One in three U.S. adults is unchurched, which translates to 65 to 70 million people.

By contrast, the church in China (both organized and underground) is growing far faster than the overall population. The same holds true for South Korea; for many African countries, from Mozambique to Nigeria; and for many countries south of our border, from Guatemala to Brazil.

According to Mission Frontiers magazine…

" • 3,000 new churches are opening every week worldwide.
 • the Church in Africa is increasing by 20,000 per day on the average.
 • worldwide, Christianity is growing at the rate of 90,000 new believers every day.
 • more Muslims in Iran have come to Christ since 1980 than in the previous thousand years combined.
 • in 1900, Korea had no Protestant church; it was deemed "impossible to penetrate." Today Korea is 35 percent Christian with 7,000 churches in the city of Seoul alone.
 • in Islamic (Muslim) Indonesia, the percentage of Christians is so high the government won't print the statistic—which is probably nearing 15 percent of the population.
 • after 70 years of oppression in Russia, people who are officially Christians number about 85 million—56 percent of the population."[12]

And Religion Today notes that
 • every day in India, 15,000 people become Christians.[13]

North America may have been the perceived leader of Christianity in past decades, but no one can make a case for that today.

IN CANADA, THE PICTURE IS JUST AS BLEAK—OR WORSE

Dr. Reginald Bibby, a researcher in the sociology of religion at the University of Lethbridge, in Alberta, Canada, has condensed his twenty-five years of research into these ten most important findings for religious leaders:

"1. Church participation is down sharply since the late 1940s. As service attendance has declined, so has personal religious commitment.

2. Few people are actually leaving. They may not be showing up all that much, but they still define themselves as being Catholic, Anglican, or Mennonite, for example.

3. Religion à la carte is rampant. External authority is out; personal authority is in.

4. Religion continues to be relational. Relationships, led by the family, are religion's centrally important transmission lines.

5. Religious memory is everywhere. Canadians who do go to church head in the direction of what is religiously familiar.

6. Receptivity to spirituality is extensive. Organized religion may be in trouble, but large numbers of Canadians who are not highly involved in a church show a remarkable openness to the supernatural and to spirituality.

7. Most people are not looking for churches. Canadians are also not in the market for religion. But they do express spiritual, personal, and social needs.

8. Most churches are not looking for people. One of the main reasons why Canada's churches are not ministering to a larger number of people is because they typically wait for people to come to them. Many Canadians are not associating their needs with churches and many churches are not associating what they have with what Canadians need.

9. Part of the problem is culture. Cultural developments, including the proliferation of choices, the increase in exposure to higher education, and the rise to prominence of electronic media as the major source of reality creation, have all had a dramatic impact on religion's role and influence.

10. The heart of the problem is churches. Churches today are collectively failing. They are well positioned to respond to the central God-self-society requirements of Canadians if they choose to do so." [14]

FACT #2: *Roughly half of all churches in America did not add one new person through conversion growth last year.*

According to denominational statistics, virtually half the churches across the United States did not record the conversion of one person last year.[15] Do these sobering figures suggest that we're not even able to keep our own children in our faith? Do they mean that the majority of newcomers to churches are simply a "circulation of the saints" [16] rather than men, women, and children who are trying to find God?

To make matters worse, other countries in the Northern Hemisphere are faring the same. University of Chicago sociologist Martin

Marty translates the trend into what happened between yesterday and today. In the part of the world that stretches west from Poland across western Europe, crosses the northern United States and Canada, and includes Japan, "there are 3,000 fewer Christians now than twenty-four hours ago, whereas in sub-Saharan Africa, there are 16,000 more Christians than twenty-four hours ago." [17]

This doesn't mean that the world missionary enterprise has decreased. The Rev. Gerald Anderson, recently retired director of the Overseas Ministries Study Center in New Haven, Connecticut, notes that it's a common misperception to think that Christian missionary activity decreased during the twentieth century.

"In fact, there are more missionaries at work today than ever before in history," he pointed out. "What has changed," Anderson says, "is at least 100,000 of these missionaries are being sent out by Protestant churches in non-Western countries." As an example, he notes that "There are now an estimated 8,000 Protestant Korean missionaries serving outside Korea." [18]

America's lack of missionary concern has reduced our fruitfulness from Times Square to Taiwan, from Iowa to Irian Jaya, from downtown to Denmark, from suburbia to the Serengeti. We're not sending many missionaries overseas anymore, much less next door.

> We're not sending many missionaries overseas anymore, much less next door.

Why? Not because we're busy preparing for a great spiritual awakening just around the corner. "If spiritual revival were occurring, you'd expect to see increasing levels of interest in a relationship with God, in church involvement, and in commitment to the Christian faith," George Barna points out. According to his research, "None of those are evident." [19]

LOCAL EVANGELISM INCLUDES AMERICA'S FIRST CITIZENS

In his article, "Awakening the Sleeping Giant," Dan Wooding writes about Christian outreach to Native Americans through Christian Hope Indian Eskimo Fellowship (CHIEF). Wooding cites evangelist Billy Graham who says, "The Native American has been like a sleeping giant. He is awakening. The original Americans could become the evangelist who will help win America for Christ!"

Huron Claus, a Mohawk Indian and fifth-generation follower of Jesus Christ, says, "I am greatly challenged, as a Native Christian, to understand why after five hundred years of evangelism among our Native American people, less than 5 percent of the total population have accepted Jesus Christ as their Lord and Savior…I believe the most effective way to reach Native Americans for Christ is when they see the examples of their own people living a life that gives God the highest praise and glory." Claus is chief executive officer of CHIEF, the organization founded by his father, Tom Claus, in 1975.

The Native American's plight today, largely triggered by terrible abuses during the conquest of America, is often as bad as the situation in developing countries. "One-third of [the] Native American population lives in poverty," notes Claus. "Unemployment on reservations varies from 40 percent to 70 percent…Adolescent suicide is approximately three times higher than national average in the age group 15 to 24 years old. Alcoholism is 5.6 times higher among Native Americans than the rest of the population of the U.S."

Wooding points out that "some 63 percent of the total Native population of 2.7 million live in the urban city areas, while most of the rest of the approximately 550 federally recognized tribes live in some 320 Indian reservations in the U.S. and 250 Alaska native villages…CHIEF has provided discipleship training, evangelism outreach, and a helps ministry for approximately 400 tribes in the Americas…[The organization] sees as one of its main roles to evangelize, disciple, mentor, and train native leaders in a culturally relevant context."

"Since 1975 at the beginning of the formation of CHIEF, the emphasis has always been to encourage and empower Native Christian leadership," Claus says.[20]

FACT #3: *No matter how you do the math, current conversion rates still point to one horrible conclusion: lost people lose.*

In America, it takes the combined efforts of eighty-five Christians working over an entire year to produce one convert.[21] At that rate, a huge percentage of people will never have the opportunity, even once, to hear the gospel from a friend they trust and in a way they can understand it.

That's not even running on fumes; it's running on empty.

If I understand my Bible correctly, the church is the only organization in society that exists for the benefit of those outside its membership. Imagine that you've been asked to consult with a group that offers the following report: "Our church has eighty-five Christians. We worked as hard as we could, employed one-tenth of our material assets, prayed diligently, and at the end of one year, we successfully developed one new convert." While you would praise God for that one, you would know that something was badly broken, horribly misaligned, and unmistakably out of order.

That those eighty-five people accept one convert as OK is even more problematic. Perhaps our indifference to the central message of our faith and the Great Commandments to love (see Matthew 22:36-39) has led many people outside the church to view us as ultimately uncaring and unreliable.

FACT #4: *Some researchers claim that more churches are closing than are opening every year.*

Almost three times as many churches in America are closing (3,750) as are opening (1,300) each year.[22] Even if the situation is not quite that bad, the net result is that there are fewer opportunities for people to encounter Christ than before.

Further, the church-to-population ratio has decreased in the last one hundred years. In 1900 the United States had 27 churches for every 10,000 people. In 1990 we were down to 12 churches per 10,000 people.[23] However, "churches are larger than they used to be, and that trend will continue," says Lyle Schaller.[24] He cites examples from various denominations to show that, for many congregations, the average size has tripled in the last one hundred years.

Yes, church congregations are, in general, bigger today; but if a great movement of God occurred, and everyone tried to go to church, we'd have nowhere to put people, even if every church ran multiple services.

FACT #5: *Conversions to other religions and dropouts from Christianity are escalating.*

Justin Long notes that in North America, "Christianity's two biggest competitors are not religious at all. From one million in 1900, the nonreligious have grown to 26 million today…Even more startling, atheists have grown from 2,000 in 1900 to 1.4 million today…Neither one of these groups shows any sign of slacking off in the near future."[25]

Here on American soil, every other religion is gaining converts while Christianity is losing them.

In addition, U.S. churches are losing at least three million people a year to secularism, consumerism, materialism, and nominalism. These "ism" words evidence themselves as people view "God as a hobby"[26] and replace church involvement with other priorities such as sports, shopping, and fixing up the house. Or they call themselves Christians simply because their culture says that they are, but not because the Word of God has grown in them (see Acts 12:24; 19:20).

In terms of faith groups here on American soil, every other religion is gaining converts while Christianity is losing them. Islam, sometimes called "the most serious threat to the church in America," [27] is growing so fast in the United States that it has either superseded Judaism as the second-largest religious group, or it's clearly in the passing lane. Between 1989 and 1998, the Muslim population in the United States grew by 25 percent, to an estimated 4 to 6 million.[28] No major American city, including those in the Bible Belt states, is without an Islamic teaching center.[29]

Christian outreach to our Muslim neighbors is almost nonexistent. There are nearly 1.2 billion Muslims worldwide, and the ratio of missionaries to Muslims is about 1 to 1 *million* globally; the ratio is even worse in North America.[30] Yet from a global perspective, Muslims, Hindus, and nonreligious people together make up about half of the world's population.[31]

Buddhism is also growing rapidly in North America. The December 1999/January 2000 issue of Civilization magazine had an entire section devoted to Buddhism entitled "Buddha Boom." [32] With more than 2.4 million adherents in North America, Buddhism is growing nearly three times as fast as Christianity.[33]

Other Eastern beliefs are also making strong inroads in North America. Best-selling author Deepak Chopra, along with others, has made Eastern views acceptable to the masses. But Eastern thought has been flowing to the West for more than a century. In 1893 at the first Parliament of World Religions in Chicago, Swami Vivekananda introduced the teachings of his Indian guru. Zen ideas were brought to the West, both by the Japanese and by Westerners who learned Zen philosophy and then returned to teach others. By the 1960s, undergraduate classes in Eastern studies were being taught at universities.[34]

The million-plus Hindus form the second-fastest growing religion in North America,[35] perhaps due to changes in immigration laws that welcome more people from Hindu-dominated countries than in the past.[36] According to a CNN news story, "Historically, most immigrants to the United States came from Europe. In 1890, for example, 86 percent were from Europe. And in 1960, Europe still accounted for 75 percent, with only 9 percent from Latin America and 5 percent from Asia. But by 1999, there had been a dramatic shift in the countries of origin of immigrants living in the United States, according to the Population Reference Bureau's Web site. In 1999 more than half—51 percent—came from Latin America and 27 percent from Asia, while only 16 percent came from Europe. This shift has brought more racial and ethnic diversity among immigrants. In 1890, only 1.4 percent of immigrants living in the United States were nonwhite. But by 1999, 75 percent were nonwhite according to the Population Reference Bureau." [37]

Christian cults that deny such basic teachings as Jesus' deity are also growing significantly, especially Jehovah's Witnesses and the Mormon church (the Church of Jesus Christ of Latter-day Saints). Their commitment to aggressive evangelism, short-term missionary service, and radical discipleship puts most Christian denominations to shame. [38]

People simply aren't sitting around waiting for churches to tell them how to "become children of God" by receiving Jesus Christ (see John 1:12). Instead they are actively seeking out other world religions and ideas such as New Age spirituality. Once people find meaning in those religions, our job of introducing them to Jesus becomes more difficult. The Holy Spirit may continue to prepare and soften their hearts, but our inaction now certainly does nothing to help soften the soil.

People may not be moving toward our Christian God, but they are becoming more spiritual. As an article in Rev. magazine notes, "Perceiving oneself to be spiritual is one of the legacies of the 90s. Seven out of ten adults now say they're spiritual. That includes nine out of ten Christians, half of the adults who don't consider themselves to be Christian, and even three out of ten atheists." [39] Yes, one-third of atheists say they are spiritual people.

O ne-third of atheists say they are spiritual people.

THE MOST WELCOME FIGURE ON THE STAGE OF WORLD RELIGION

To his followers, "the Dalai Lama *is* a buddha." Kenneth Woodward, writing in Newsweek magazine, continues: "Ten years after he won the Nobel Prize for Peace, Tenzin Gyatso has become unofficial lama to the world. His is the face that Buddhism wears, especially in the West...He [taught] Buddhist meditation to sold-out crowds in New York City and [gave] a free public lecture in the East Meadow of Central Park. One of his three dozen books, *The Art of Happiness*, [was] on The New York Times bestseller list for twenty-nine weeks."

Woodward goes on to say, "His encompassing smile...his engaging humility and nonjudgmental manner have made the Dalai Lama the most benign and welcome figure on the stage of world religion...The Dalai Lama has been an eloquent promoter of religious understanding. He has offered a Buddhist commentary on the gospel to Catholic monks...and urged his own monks to emulate 'my Christian brothers and sisters' in transforming Buddhist compassion into concrete acts of social service."

In the Dalai Lama, "Buddhism couldn't find a more persuasive face." [40]

PAGANISM, IVY LEAGUE-STYLE

"Pagan groups are growing in popularity on college campuses. In Massachusetts, according to The Boston Globe, there are more than seven student pagan groups at schools like Amherst, Wellesley, Smith, Boston University, Northeastern, Emerson, and Berklee. Pagans at MIT recently celebrated a Halloween ritual in the chapel where they knelt before an altar somberly chanting, 'Dark mother take us in...Let us be reborn.'Then they walked under a dark veil that represented the underworld and ate pomegranate seeds and danced barefoot in a circle. 'It's natural for college students to be attracted to things they haven't thought or experienced before,' said Christine Thomas, a religion professor at the University of California at Santa Barbara. 'But this movement is a reflection of a lot of things: fascination with the occult, the lack of one religion's hegemony, and the explosion of information and networking opportunities available on the Internet.'" [41]

FACT #6: *The decline in Christianity has been going on for nearly fifty years.*

The explosion of megachurches and other fast-growing congregations has masked the impact of an overall discouraging and negative trend: In the past fifty years, U.S. churches have failed to gain an additional 2 percent of the American population. [42]

Regular church attendance once characterized the dominant half of the population, but today more North Americans are outside the church than inside it, in terms of regular attendance. The U.S. attendance figure, which many researchers think is optimistic,[43] is about 40 percent on any given week.

Today more North Americans are outside the church than inside it.

American religion is weakening, according to social researcher Robert Putnam. In his book, *Bowling Alone: The Collapse and Revival of American Community*, he documents that church membership and attendance have declined by as much as 10 percent since the 1960s. He goes on to explain that the breakdown of community is not just a hunch of social commentators, but a sociological fact with severe consequences. [44]

While it's true that overall U.S. church membership has steadily increased over the last two centuries,[45] and taken a dip in the last decade, membership means nothing if you don't show up. That's like trying to win an athletic event by remaining seated in the stands. It's like joining a health club and expecting to get in shape without ever getting off the couch.

FACT #7: *Too many churched people believe and behave identically to their unchurched counterparts.*

The belief system of a huge number of churchgoers is dangerously at odds with the faith of the first church led by Jesus' apostles and recorded in the New Testament. For example: What would you call a person who believes in astrology, reincarnation, and the possibility of communicating with the dead? If your first thought is "New Ager," you missed an important group. According to a Gallup survey, these are just some of the beliefs held by people who call themselves Christians.[46]

> The belief system of a huge number of churchgoers is dangerously at odds with the faith of the first church led by Jesus' apostles.

Gallup's survey reveals a shocking fact: An awful lot of people who call themselves Christians haven't a clue what Christianity is all about. They've adopted what University of California scholar Wade Clark Roof calls a "salad bar" approach to their faith: Just pick and choose the spiritual beliefs you like, add a dash of God, and consider yourself a Christian. That's the American Christian of the new millennium.

Sociologist Robert Bellah predicted this development almost twenty years ago in his bestseller *Habits of the Heart*. He identified the tendency of many Christians to modify and dilute biblical ideas so that Jesus is seen as a friend who helps us on the road to happiness and self-fulfillment.[47]

This "religion of me and thee," as George Gallup, Jr., calls it,[48] along with a hunger for experience over knowledge, has contributed to a tremendous diversity of beliefs, many of which are antithetical to biblical principles. These unhealthy attitudes have crept into the church, as evidenced by the following results of a survey of church lay leaders by researcher George Barna[49]:

• only 53 percent believe that there are moral truths that are absolute.

    • 43 percent say there is no such thing as the Holy Spirit.

    • 33 percent believe that Jesus never had a physical resurrection.

    • 19 percent believe Jesus sinned while on earth.

Not only are the beliefs of Christians often at odds with the teaching of their churches, but also behavioral differences are often nonexistent between the churched and the unchurched. This comparison suggests that whatever is happening inside the church is having zero effect on behavior in day-to-day living.

Sometimes behavior by those who profess Christ is actually worse than those who don't. For example, despite increased concern about national morality, Christians continue to have a higher likelihood of getting divorced than do non-Christians. Even atheists are less likely to become divorced than are Christians.[50]

Despite its Christian heritage, the United States leads every other nation in the industrialized world in the percentage of single-parent families (at 23 percent),[51] abortion rate (at 22.9 per 1,000 women aged 15-44),[52] sexually transmitted diseases (syphilis rate is 6.3 per 100,000 and gonorrhea rate is 149.5 per 100,000),[53] teenage birth rate (42 per 1,000 girls aged 15-19),[54] use of illegal drugs by students (44.9 percent using in 1998),[55] and the size of the prison population (327 per 100,000).[56] Our rate of child poverty (20 percent) is likewise abysmal.[57]

Where is the church's positive impact on individuals and society? At stake is the deadly assumption that business as usual is just fine. It's even more deadly when churches aren't even aware that they've made such an assumption. We impact one life here and another one there, and we wrongly assume that as other churches do likewise, we're making forward progress.

The exact opposite is true. Churches are going out of business. Why? Because they refuse to change. They're like the proverbial frog placed in a slowly warming pot of water. The frog gets cooked because it doesn't notice and doesn't respond to the changes around it.

Any church that doesn't shift from "ministry as status quo" to "ministry as mission field" will die or it becomes hopelessly irrelevant to the people its charter document—the Bible—calls it to love, serve, reach, and even die for.

WHAT DOES IT MEAN?

The problem of insular, unchanging, and increasingly irrelevant churches isn't a financial one. Although people who claim the name of Christ constitute 32 percent of the world's population, they receive 62 percent of the world's yearly income and spend 97 percent of their resources on themselves.[58] According to George Barna, "they spend roughly twice as much money on entertainment as they donate to their church." [59]

And the problem is not due to a lack of education or a lack of good information. Literacy and educational levels among North American Christians are at an all-time high. The 1998 Consumer Research Study

Book Purchasing shows that, in the United States during 1998, more than 10 million religious books were purchased—that's about 10 percent of all adult books sold.[60] In 2000 alone, more than 8,000 titles were printed by Christian publishers.[61] By contrast, half the world is waiting for its first Bible. "More than 3 billion people have yet to own a Bible," claims an ad for the American Bible Society.[62]

Nor is the problem due to the government's barring the Bible from public schools and banning student-led prayer from athletic fields. Unlike countries such as Iraq, Cuba, or China, the United States does not tell churches what we can or cannot teach our people. We may have to pay taxes to buy our Bibles and training materials, but we are free to change how we do church—whenever we want to.

The inescapable conclusion is that we must throw out any notion that God is truly at the center of the church's heart in North America. Maybe we're blessed with bigger incomes, but by every other standard, most Christians around the world outshine us. (And many of them out-tithe us as well, with the average American churchgoer giving only 2.56 percent of his or her 1997 income, an 18 percent decrease from 1968.)[63]

We must throw out any notion that God is truly at the center of the church's heart in North America.

Instead, the church of tomorrow must not look like the church of today. To be what God has called us to be, tomorrow's church needs to look and behave more like the first-century church than the twentieth-century church, as Bill Easum often says.

The next chapters of *Lost in America* show how you—as part of a church—can find and participate in what God is doing to restore a vital Christianity in your community.

WHAT PART OF "GO" DON'T WE UNDERSTAND?

The end of the Bible affirms that God's people are on the winning side. The Bible tells Christians to go into all the world beginning in their own communities. In what is known as the Great Commission—Jesus' last known instructions to his followers—Jesus gave his charge: "God authorized and commanded me to commission you: Go out and train everyone you meet, far and near, in this way of life, marking them by baptism in the threefold name: Father, Son, and Holy Spirit. Then instruct them in the practice of all I have commanded you. I'll be with you as you do this, day after day after day, right up to the end of the age" (Matthew 28:18-20, *The Message*).

I contend that we're losing the battle and don't even realize it. The only realistic solution is for the church to reposition itself to reach this continent again. The time of small thinking and small vision must end.

Christians must reproduce Christians, and churches must reproduce churches.

We can no longer afford to sit still, waiting for people to come to us. We must go into the world and be Christians who reproduce Christians and churches that reproduce churches. The Apostle Paul told a friend, "I pray that you may be active in sharing your faith, so that you will have a full understanding of every good thing we have in Christ" (Philemon 1:6).

The starting point for building the kind of intentional relationships that enable you to make a difference is realizing that you and your church must change—that most congregations and denominations have lost their sense of purpose, their focus, and their primary calling. Even if our words affirm that lost people really do matter to God, our behavior too often denies that life-changing truth.

That's not the way things have to be. During the Apollo 13 mission, NASA's team would not accept failure and instead achieved its finest hour. Over the last couple of years I have met and talked with a huge number of Christians who are discouraged because their church isn't going anywhere. They are quick to acknowledge that things are not right, but they are too discouraged to try to think of alternatives. They don't believe that the near future can be the church's finest hour. People in those churches hear so much negative information about the world and receive so little hope or encouragement accompanied with concrete ideas to break the apathy.

My prayer is that this book will be a tool God uses to break the apathy, encourage you, and provoke you to make a difference starting right where you are. As the Bible says, "Let us consider how we may spur one another on toward love and good deeds" (Hebrews 10:24).

RENT THIS MOVIE

The Perfect Storm
(Action/Adventure, PG-13)

A commercial fishing-boat crew, desperate for economic success, sets out to fish the fertile waters of the North Atlantic. As the five fishermen try to return home with their record haul, in denial of reality and blinded by their own ambitions, they head straight into the worst, most ferocious storm in history.

What to look for: Just like Jonah, asleep in the bottom of the boat and running away from what God wanted him to do, many churches, also desperate for survival but in denial of reality, are headed straight into a hurricane of cultural upheaval and social isolation that threatens to destroy them. Yet these churches refuse to awaken from their fitful slumber. How did this movie make you feel about why the men went into the storm and what happened to them?

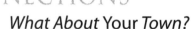

CONNECTIONS

What About Your *Town?*

If you're hoping that your community is an exception to the statistics presented in this chapter, try the following suggestions:

1. Go to a nearby bookstore in your community and try to find out whether people are buying more New Age books or books about a relationship with God through Jesus Christ.

2. Look in the Yellow Pages of your phone directory under "churches" and "religious organizations." What percentage would you guess do not teach the gospel of Jesus Christ as revealed in Scripture and taught by your church?

3. Go to a public place like a nearby garage sale or shopping mall and try to tally how many different languages you hear spoken by shoppers over the course of an hour. Or visit a restaurant and notice what language the workers and other customers around you are speaking. Then ask longtime Christians in your community how many churches they can think of that reach out to those specific language groups. ("Well, there's the Korean Presbyterian church, the Assemblies of God Spanish-language church, and the Baptist-sponsored Russian congregation.") Does your tally of the different languages you heard fall far short of the number of language-sensitive churches?

4. Arrange to ride the midnight shift with a local police officer. Think about who is reaching this whole different population that lives and works at night.

Discussion Questions

1. What stood out to you most in this chapter? Why?

2. Is the concept of the United States of America as a mission field easy or difficult for you to grasp? Why or why not?

3. What feelings do you have toward being a missionary to America?

4. What makes you want to see the church do a better job of impacting our culture?

5. What are some issues you should be praying about as a result of reading this chapter?

CHAPTER 3

PEOPLE ARE DIFFERENT

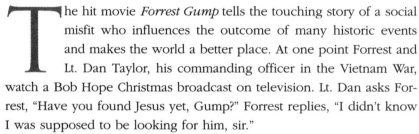

Three needs unlock the doors that allow you to enter into deeper relationships with those who do not yet have a personal faith relationship with Jesus Christ.

The hit movie *Forrest Gump* tells the touching story of a social misfit who influences the outcome of many historic events and makes the world a better place. At one point Forrest and Lt. Dan Taylor, his commanding officer in the Vietnam War, watch a Bob Hope Christmas broadcast on television. Lt. Dan asks Forrest, "Have you found Jesus yet, Gump?" Forrest replies, "I didn't know I was supposed to be looking for him, sir."

People today may not understand our church phrases, but they're certainly asking "our" questions. In the course of telling his story, Forrest deals with humanity's deepest issues of love and hate, fear and courage, and life and death. He prays and goes to church, but he doesn't find answers he can comprehend. Instead, his mother speaks the language he understands best.

"What's my destiny, Momma?" Forrest once asked her.

"You're gonna have to figure that out for yourself," she replied, "Life is a box of chocolates, Forrest. You never know what you're gonna get."

"Momma always had a way of explaining things so I could understand them," concluded Forrest.

PEOPLE ARE LOOKING ANYWHERE AND EVERYWHERE FOR SPIRITUAL ANSWERS

Many people are desperately seeking spiritual meaning in life. In the past, people thought of church as the place to go if they were looking for spiritual meaning. Not so today. Now people are willing to go anywhere for it. Whether through New Age channeling or chat rooms on the Internet, people are finding ways to fill the spiritual void in their lives and answer their internal questions about purpose and meaning. This opportunity is what "status quo" churches are missing, if by status quo we mean churches that have ceased to reach out beyond their members.

I n the past, people thought of church as the place to go if they were looking for spiritual meaning. Not so today.

The evening that my friend, Warren Bird, edited this chapter, he took a break to channel surf on television. On one channel, CBS ran the second part of *Jesus*, its most popular miniseries of the season—a $17 million project. The first part of the miniseries was the first program to top a Sunday episode of *Who Wants to Be a Millionaire*. On another channel, CNN's *Larry King Live* featured an interview with best-selling author Deepak Chopra about his recent book, *How to Know God*. During the interview, King announced that his guest the next night would be Billy Graham's daughter, Anne Graham Lotz, to talk about her newest book, *Just Give Me Jesus*.

The Indwelling: The Beast Takes Possession, the seventh book in the overtly religious "Left Behind" series by Tim LaHaye and Jerry Jenkins, reached first place on The New York Times fiction bestseller list in June 2000. An article in The Times called the book "an unparalleled achievement for an evangelical novel." In the first month alone, the book sold two million copies. "This is a phenomenal number of books we're talking about," said Daisy Maryles, executive editor of Publishers Weekly.[1] The authors of *The Indwelling*, who say they have made more than $10 million each from the series, are far more excited about the thousands of people who report that they've become Christians because of the book. "To us, that's the most satisfying part of this entire experience— others coming to Christ," Jenkins says.[2]

Ten years ago, that level of positive secular coverage of spiritual issues would have been unimaginable. Today it's everywhere, from Joan Osborne's hit song "One of Us" in which she asks "What if God was one of us?" to Dr. Laura Schlessinger's daily radio broadcast in which she gives hard-hitting advice about values, principles, ethics, and faith issues.[3]

T en years ago, that level of positive secular coverage of spiritual issues would have been unimaginable.

IS TODAY SO DIFFERENT FROM THE 1960S?

"From local papers to the Web, the press has responded with more religion news than at any time in decades," reports a story in The Christian

Science Monitor. "Stories about everything from prayer groups to reincarnation to African-based ancestor worship have replaced what thirty years ago was primarily the domain of bake sales and church notices."

The article goes on to say, "In the past decade, many newspapers have added sections devoted to faith and values and reporters to go with them. Newsmagazines now regularly feature religious subjects on their covers—and do brisk business when they do. Religion news is also increasing on the Internet, and to a lesser extent on TV and the radio."[4]

What a contrast to the turbulent 1960s when John Lennon, the man best known for the lines "Imagine there's no heaven/It's easy if you try" was living a life dictated by astrologers, numerologists, clairvoyants, psychics, herbalists, and tarot-card readers. Or is it such a change?

PEOPLE'S HOT BUTTONS HAVE CHANGED

Many longtime Christians have become discouraged by sagging church attendance and the loss of Judeo-Christian values at work, at school, and in American culture as a whole. The decline is real and undeniable.

The problem is not a lack of spiritual hunger or interest. Instead, people's response points have changed. What worked effectively in the past doesn't necessarily connect with society nowadays. Yesteryear's appeal to guilt or duty doesn't resonate well today, and institutional loyalty is at an all-time low. Fear of dangling in hell

Yesteryear's appeal to guilt or duty doesn't resonate well today.

doesn't impact people because most seekers aren't even sure hell exists, and they are turned off by negative threats.

Besides, the here and now is so pleasant and comfortable that, to most Americans, the idea of eternal life has little urgency. The great abundance of the 1950s couldn't satisfy Americans so, in the 1960s and 1970s, people dabbled in drugs, protests, and free love. Those decades left Americans so empty and lost that they dove headfirst into the consumerism, hedonism, and extravagance of the 1980s. The economic boom resulting from the powerful investing of the 1980s drove the U.S. economy to heights never before seen. These kinds of values and events have significantly shaped popular culture.

In terms of lifestyle, most Americans are doing better today than ever before. But people seem less satisfied than ever. Today there are unprecedented spiritual yearnings and desires as Americans of the baby boomer generation struggle with their own mortality and prepare for their own deaths. At the same time, succeeding generations are coping with their personal pain and disillusionment in life. All of these struggles provide golden opportunities for the church, but people are looking for eternal solutions elsewhere.

Further, while Americans are deeply religious, they're generally not acquainted with or committed to the teachings of whatever faith they claim. According to sociologist Alan Wolfe, "Americans take their religion seriously. But very few of them take it so seriously that they believe that religion should be the sole, or even the most important, guide for establishing rules about how *other* people should live. And some...also would distrust such rules for providing guidelines about how they personally should live."[5]

> **Life's struggles provide golden opportunities for the church, but people are looking for eternal solutions elsewhere.**

PEOPLE RESPOND WHEN YOU MEET THREE NEEDS

People are interested in issues, causes, and activities that match their own needs and interests. In that regard, three hot buttons *do* generate a response today. People come to earth with three fundamental needs—transcendence, significance, and community. Most felt needs today can be traced to one of these three sources.

Searching for a Divine Relationship

First, we need **transcendence**. Everyone, at some point in life, wants to know God—to know the mystical and the divine, to solve the dilemma of life's God-shaped vacuum, and to know the great beyond.

Nine of the ten all-time, top-grossing films have a clear supernatural theme.[6] And most of literature's great epic stories deal with the human quest for God.

In their hit song "I Still Haven't Found What I'm Looking For," the rock band U2 expresses the search for transcendence in their lyrics, "I have climbed the highest mountains...but I still haven't found what I'm looking for." In "Losing My Religion," R.E.M. sings about a similar theme: "Life is bigger/It's bigger than you/and you are not me...Oh no, I've said too much/I haven't said enough." So does Creed, whose song "Higher," asks, "Can you take me higher/to a place where blind men see?/Can you take me higher/to the place with golden streets?"

In every corner of today's popular culture, people are asking questions about transcendence. Sensitivity to that yearning can help you enter into deeper relationships with those who do not yet have a personal faith relationship with Jesus Christ. In their more reflective moments, people agree with Saint Augustine who said, "You awake us to delight in your presence; for you made us for yourself, and our heart is restless until it rests in you."[7]

Questions of Meaning and Purpose

Second, people seek **significance**. They want a purpose in life—to feel that they're doing something meaningful, to feel empowered to do something important, and to have a reason to get out of bed in the morning.

I travel some 250,000 miles each year, and I have many opportunities to talk to people across the United States and even in other countries. As I meet different men and women, I enjoy thinking about the "significance question": What makes life worth living for this person?

No matter where I am or who I'm with, I consistently observe that people have a deep-seated longing for a life that has purpose. Most of the people I talk with try to find meaning in one of two ways: through money or experiences. When I talk with people who are pursuing money, they freely admit that their drive is not so much for more money as for the meaning in life they hope it will create. Somehow if they have enough money—usually defined as "just a little more than I currently have"—they'll arrive at that point. Or so they believe. People who seek experiences describe similar desired and predicted outcomes.

I'll always remember a Fortune 500 power broker I once met on an airplane. Listening to his story of wealth, fame, influence, and broken relationships, he sounded like the poster child for the American dream. I would get a C minus at best on his scale of success. Yet he dropped several hints that his life felt hollow. After he listened to my passion to help people reach their potential through Jesus Christ, he looked me in the eye and said sincerely, "I would give anything to do something so meaningful."

AMERICANS ASK SPIRITUAL QUESTIONS ABOUT MEANING IN LIFE

According to a Charisma News Service article, America remains one of the highest-ranked nations in terms of reflection on the meaning and purpose of life. That conclusion is based in part on the results of a poll conducted by the University of Michigan's Institute for Social Research.

While more people are searching for spiritual answers, they aren't necessarily looking for those answers at church. "Although church attendance is declining in nearly all advanced industrial societies, spiritual concerns more broadly defined are not," notes Ronald Inglehart, who was one of the authors of the study. "In fact, in most industrial societies, a growing share of the population is spending time thinking about the meaning and purpose of life."

The article reports that "Questions about the meaning and purpose of life grew most markedly in the advanced industrial democracies of Australia, West Germany, South Korea, Italy, and the Netherlands. In the United States, 46 percent of those questioned said that they thought about the meaning and purpose of life 'often.'" [8]

It Takes a Village to Become Fully Human

The third need is for **community**—to connect with other people through meaningful relationships. Most people could make it in life without riches or toys, but few, if any, could survive without friends and a sense of family.

Kyle, whose dad was a pastor, had heard the gospel hundreds of times. He didn't lack the right information. My wife and I got to know Kyle when we began leading a Christian education class for young families at our church. After one of our times together, I asked Kyle and his wife, along with another couple, "Are you satisfied with your life as Christians?" Both wives said no.

Later, over a snack at Dairy Queen, Kyle admitted, "I don't have *any* kind of spiritual life. I come to church because I think it's the right thing to do, but I've seen too much junk and been too disillusioned to take it seriously."

I suspected that seeing others live the gospel and participating in community were the only things that would connect with Kyle. My wife and I formed a small group with these two couples.

We'd hire a babysitter to watch over the seven kids (newborn through age nine) from three families. We'd set the timer for half an hour. Then we'd read from the gospel according to Mark and talk about it until the bell rang. We'd reset the timer for another half an hour and talk about where we were in life. Finally we'd pray about whatever we had discussed. Through these weekly meetings, we came to care for and trust one another.

Unknown to us, Kyle and Brianna's marriage was on the rocks. His business was going great, and he was on top of the world everywhere but at home. It got so bad that Brianna asked Kyle to move out.

I first learned of their problem on Valentine's Day. After a nice evening with my wife, we were getting ready for bed when the phone rang. It was Kyle, asking if he could come over.

We sat in the kitchen, drank coffee, and talked. He wanted a quick fix, and he was far more interested in seeing his wife change than in making a change himself. He was viewing God more as "the Divine Fix-It" than as Savior and Lord.

One evening a few days later, the other couple in our group was at our house playing a board game. The phone rang. It was Kyle. I didn't even recognize his voice at first because of his emotional state. "I wanted you to be the first to know that I'm giving my life to Jesus Christ," he said.

"That's great," I replied, mentioning that the other couple was already at my house. "Why don't you come over?"

"I realized that God doesn't love me based on how good I've been," Kyle continued. "For the first time in my life, from what we've been talking about from the book of Mark, I understand about the grace of God. He loves me for who I am." Kyle spent a long time unraveling for us the performance issues that had arrested his spiritual development. But now he had truly discovered how Christ could be at the center of his life.

Unfortunately, his marriage had unraveled too far. Kyle's wife had picked up many of Kyle's bad habits, and he'd pulled her down. "I don't want this now," she told him and us. Instead of starting over with Kyle, she turned elsewhere for love and support.

Kyle had been told the right words all his life, but something had kept him from hearing. He discovered what he needed from the Word of God and in community.

FROM JESUS TO THE EARLY CHURCH

Jesus' ministry appealed to these three needs. His core message appealed to transcendence: "The kingdom of God is near. Repent and believe the good news!" (Mark 1:15). His call to Peter and Andrew, " 'Come, follow me,' Jesus said, 'and I will make you fishers of men' " (Mark 1:17), could be understood as a call to significance because he would give the disciples something extremely worthwhile to do with their fishing skills. Jesus began his public ministry by identifying with the greater community of faith through his baptism (see Mark 1:5-11; Matthew 3:13-17), and by building what today we'd call a small-group community of the twelve apostles with the inner core of Peter, James, and John.

The book of Acts records the first years of the early church. It, too, points to these three needs. The life of the early church epitomized a transcendent relationship, a purpose with significance, and an identity found in community. All three qualities can be found, for example, in the very first description of the early church, Acts 2:42-47, as people worshipped and prayed to God, reached out to others, and grew into a fellowship.

Various conversion accounts in Acts also point to how these needs were met. The Ethiopian eunuch in Acts 8:26-39 was a man of great stature, wealth, and power. Yet none of that had satisfied his longings. As he traveled in his chariot, he was trying to understand a story about life and death from the Scriptures. He sought transcendence. Paul Johnson, author of such bestsellers as *Modern Times* and *A History of the Jews*, affirms this search: "Perhaps the greatest merit of Christianity is that…it offers an antidote to the fear death arouses in us, a firm promise of another world beyond, and the means to enter it.[9]

The need for significance shows up in many places, such as in Paul's conversion as he learns that he's been called to God for a new purpose in life: "You will be his witness to all men of what you have seen and heard" (Acts 22:15). He devoted the rest of his life to that destiny.

We can see the need for community in the conversion of many men and women. The narrative from Acts 4:32–5:14 describes the authentic biblical community of mutual concern, charity, and sacrifice. Coupled with the powerful demonstration of the Spirit's convicting power, this sense of community led to an incredible purification and subsequent increase in the early church as "more and more men and women believed in the Lord and were added to their number" (Acts 5:14).

Even the Holy Trinity represents these three needs. The Father's call invites us into transcendence, the Son's commission offers us significance, and the Holy Spirit's comfort draws us together as community. Could it be that humanity's three deepest needs are exactly met by the Trinity?

CLOSE & PERSONAL

Meeting People at Their Point of Need or Pain

Few churches in America today exhibit a story as remarka̶
of New Hope Community Church in Portland, Ore̶

beginnings in a drive-in theater in 1972 to today's beautiful campus along a busy interstate highway, God has used the church to heal tens of thousands of hurting people.

"One of our earliest values was to heal hurts and build dreams," says Dale Galloway, the founding pastor. That value attracted all kinds of individuals who needed emotional and spiritual healing. It also attracted Christians with the spiritual gift of mercy who wanted to help.

Even during the church's first days when Dale and his wife Margi sang and preached from the roof of a snack shack at a drive-in theater, they laid plans for need-meeting ministries that would reach the unchurched people of Portland. Week after week, Galloway told the small congregation, "Some day we'll have small groups all over the city led by dedicated laypeople. Some day we'll have at least a hundred different need-meeting ministries that heal hurts and build dreams right where people are."

The church's many ministries grew out of a series of small groups that the Galloways launched. While the public beginning of New Hope occurred at a drive-in theater, in reality the church started with one small group that met in a home. "Out of that we created the next groups, and out of those came leaders for many other groups," says Galloway. Four of New Hope's staff pastors emerged from those early groups. Their first ministry had been to lead a small group.

"We discovered firsthand that small groups were a highly effective way to reach unchurched people, so we created different kinds of groups targeted to meet people either at their point of need or interest," explains Galloway. They sponsored nurture groups called Tender Loving Care groups, task groups, support-and-recovery groups, fellowship groups, and special-interest groups. These cells became an entry point through which many people connected to God, to each other, and to the church. Some 80 percent of them had never belonged to a church before.

"Year after year we demonstrated that the more need-meeting ministries you have, the more people you will reach," Galloway notes. "...ple at their point of need or pain and you'll have no shortage ... When you reach out to people in a meaningful way, they will

...re lay pastors the church developed, the more the church's ... love multiplied. "I could never give that amount or level of ... I were personally available twenty-four hours a day, seven ..." Galloway says. "New Hope's network of care emerged only as I multiplied myself through others."

The church, pastored by Ray Cotton since 1995, continues to be a community of lives transformed through the power of Jesus Christ. "As long as there are people with hurts and needs, we'll be reaching out to them," affirms Cotton.

POPCORN EVANGELISM

Invite some friends over to watch the movies described in the "Rent This Movie" sections of this book, and talk about the movies afterward. Raise questions that invite discussions about transcendence, significance, and community.

Movies matter so much today, according to Charles Henderson, organizing pastor of the First Church of Cyberspace, because they "are one of the most revealing signals of what is happening in American culture. Our movies often reveal the central hopes and fears of people who are trying to make their way through these confusing times." [10]

Another approach is to talk about popular songs. Think about a memorable line, and start a discussion. For example, you might say, "I've been thinking about the song 'Lucky' by Britney Spears. She sings, 'If there's nothing missing in my life, then why do these tears come at night?' What do you think is missing for her?"

MAKE SURE THESE NEEDS ARE MET IN YOUR OWN LIFE

Jesus taught "No one can come to me unless the Father who sent me draws him" (John 6:44). I believe the three needs are like powerful magnets drawing us to God. Our job is to cooperate with the way in which God is drawing us to him.

The starting point is to realize that we all want to have these needs met. The next step is to make sure that I have allowed all three fundamental needs to be met in me through Jesus Christ.

When I recognize that these three dominant needs are in me, in you, and in everyone else, and when I yield to my Savior to meet those needs in my life, then I'm equipped and empowered to be more effective in evangelism. This reality will be demonstrated in every one of my relationships, such as in my relationship with my friend, Charles.

I met Charles, a massive, barrel-chested man with tender spirit, through a historic re-enactment club. We've become good friends over the years, and our wives have become friends, too.

Charles tells me that when he's with his friends in the club, "it's like a large nondenominational church." He has closer fellowship than at any church he could imagine, he says. If he has a need, he can pick up the phone at any time of day or night and people who care will come right over. Who could ask for more? He has a need for community, but as he views his life right now, that need is already being met.

How about the search for significance? Charles' career as a pre-school teacher is an important, but not prestigious, line of work. Interestingly, he's found an important role through his hobbies. He holds a very respected regional position in a national voluntary organization. So he's not searching for significance right now either.

Charles' unmet need at present is for transcendence. He and I were together just after he learned about the death of a dear friend who was killed in a car accident. "How can I make sense of this?" he asked me. "Her death is going to devastate our group." His questions to me such as, "How do I make it through this loss?" help me know that he's looking for hope. They suggest that he's not able to find answers to eternal questions.

As Charles and I talked, tears welled up in the eyes of this big, burly man. "You're unlike any other religious person I know," he said. "I normally freak out when people talk about religion, but with you it's real life."

Why would he say that? How did we get to that point in our relationship?

First, we wouldn't communicate on that level unless we had already built a meaningful relationship. I don't care about him in order to convert him. He's not my "project"; he's one of my very best friends.

I genuinely like and enjoy Charles, and he knows it. He knows that I pray regularly for him, starting long ago when he told me about the ringing in his ears that doctors couldn't solve. "I've been praying for your ear problem," I told him later.

He's not my "project"; he's one of my very best friends.

Even after the situation with his ears improved, Charles told me, "Don't stop praying for me." So I've prayed for him about other concerns, both physical and spiritual. Over the months of our friendship, I've sensed that God is drawing Charles closer, although the road has been difficult. As a result, I have wept more in prayer for Charles than I have in praying for anyone else in a long time.

Our ongoing relationship illustrates how anyone, if he or she is simply aware of these needs that everyone has, can become a mc

giving witness. By cooperating with the Holy Spirit, who is c **52**

people like Charles to God, I can be used by God just by being

Evangelism isn't about trying to use gifts you don't have; it's being genuine and authentic about yourself. Charles knows me—with my warts, dysfunctions, and goof-ups. He recognizes the presence of God at work in me through all of it.

> **Evangelism isn't about trying to use gifts you don't have; it's being genuine and authentic about yourself.**

My favorite acronym for grace is **G**od's **R**ighteousness **A**nd **C**orresponding **E**nablement. By grace, the Holy Spirit empowers you and me to be effective witnesses. Our worlds are full of people like Charles who are watching and are willing to experience more of God for themselves.

Ministry occurs in ongoing relationships more than in church buildings. Today's change in hot buttons provides a golden opportunity for us to enter the world of others and show them how Jesus Christ is sufficient to meet all of their needs. We serve a God who promises to "meet all your needs according to his glorious riches in Christ Jesus" (Philippians 4:19).

> **Ministry occurs in ongoing relationships more than in church buildings.**

People today can be reached. Are you willing to change your approach in order to start where they are? Are you willing to let God change your life first by meeting all your needs?

RENT THIS MOVIE

Star Wars: Episode I—The Phantom Menace
(Science Fiction, PG)

A galactic trade dispute sends a Jedi Master and his apprentice as ambassadors on a diplomatic mission. They must rescue a queen from an android invasion, and they encounter numerous challenges on their journeys. Along the way, they meet a child slave named Anakin, in whom the Force is very powerful. The Jedi Master wants Anakin to become a Jedi, but other Jedis sense something unsettling about the boy.

What to look for: What motivates Anakin? In what ways does he indicate a need for significance (such as in his desire to go from a slave to a Jedi), transcendence (in wanting to learn about the Force), and community (in his response to mentors and friends)? How are his needs similar to those of people today?

CONNECTIONS

How Would You Write This Book for Your City?

Unreached Mega Peoples of India, published by India Missions Association, describes one hundred different groups, including occupational castes and religious groups, each with over one million people.[11]

1. Suppose you tried to create the same kind of book about the people of your city. What groups of people or sections of town would you describe as the primary unreached groups in *your* area?

2. Of the three human needs discussed in this chapter—transcendence, significance, and community—which one is the easiest and most natural for *you* to talk about?

3. Describe a time someone addressed one of those three needs in *your* life.

4. Which of the needs do you want to become more aware of in others, such as in the group you named above? What kind of question would a person in that group be most interested in, and why?

Discussion Questions

1. To what extent do you agree or disagree that these three needs—transcendence, significance, and community—are valid ways for reaching your family and friends?

2. How can an increased awareness of these needs help you to become a more effective witness?

3. The need most often addressed in typical evangelistic efforts is transcendence. How can focusing on only one need lead to an unbalanced view for people who have not yet become open to having a relationship with Christ?

4. Which, if any, of the three needs are not currently being met in your life? How can you begin to let God address this need?

Optional: List examples from Scripture in which these three needs are addressed.

CHAPTER 4

THE WORLD IS DIFFERENT

Today's world has shifted Christianity and churches from the mainstream to the margins of society.

The popular movie *The Matrix* begins with the hero living a relatively ordinary life in what he thinks is the year 1999. By day, the potential savior of the world is computer programmer Thomas Anderson. By night he's a computer hacker with the online name of Neo.

Then a man named Morpheus shows up. Morpheus wears a long black coat and his eyes are hidden behind mirrored sunglasses. With his Cheshire-cat, enigmatic smile, he explains that in reality it's actually two hundred years later, after the world has been wasted and taken over by forms of advanced artificial intelligence. The supercomputers with human-looking programs have created a false version of twentieth-century life called the Matrix to keep their human slaves satisfied and deceived.

Neo shakes himself, as if trying to wake up from a bizarre dream.

"Do you believe in fate, Neo?" Morpheus asks.

Neo indicates no.

"Why not?" asks Morpheus.

"Because I don't like the idea that I'm not in control of my life," replies Neo.

Morpheus explains that Neo is not in control because of the Matrix. "You feel it when you go to work, or go to church, or pay your taxes. It is the world that has been pulled over your eyes to blind you from the truth."

"What truth?" asks Neo.

"That you are a slave, Neo," Morpheus tells him. "Like everyone else, you were born into bondage, kept inside a prison that you cannot smell, taste, or touch. A prison for your mind. Unfortunately, no one can be told what the Matrix is. You have to see it for yourself."

Red Pill or Blue Pill?

Morpheus then offers Neo the choice of two pills.

"This is your last chance," Morpheus warns Neo. "After this, there is no going back. You take the blue pill and the story ends. You wake up in your bed and believe whatever you want to believe."

Neo studies the pills in Morpheus' open hands. In the right is a red pill. In the left, a blue pill.

Morpheus continues by making a reference to Lewis Carroll's *Alice in Wonderland*, after Alice tumbled through the rabbit hole. "You take the red pill and you stay in Wonderland, and I show you how deep the rabbit hole goes…Remember that all I am offering is the truth. Nothing more."

Neo swallows the red pill, and Morpheus' smile returns. The chase begins as Neo is hailed as "The One" to lead the remaining real humans to overthrow the machines and reclaim the earth.

Reality Ain't What It Used to Be

Previous generations would not have given much credibility to a movie like *The Matrix*. Who would seriously believe that someone could travel back and forth between the world of reality and the artificial, dreamlike illusion of virtual reality, as Neo does?

Yet *The Matrix* is popular because in today's postmodern world, people aren't as sure about the nature of reality as they once were. They are open to many interpretations, even some that others might find illogical or absurd.

P**eople aren't as sure about the nature of reality as they once were.**

According to the story line, Neo wants to learn by experiencing true reality even if reality isn't what he thought it to be. In fact, what he thought was reality isn't even real. It's a computer-generated illusion to keep people from rebelling against the machines that actually run the world.

Morpheus invites Neo into the story. His narrative speaks to the intrinsic desire people have to explain the hurt, pain, and confusion in their lives. Neo's response affirms the human desire for significance—to be a part of something meaningful—as the previous chapter discussed.

Each person in today's world faces a choice similar to Neo's choice between the red and blue pills. If you don't follow Christ, you might still enjoy a fairly comfortable life in this world. Like someone taking the blue pill, many people in today's affluent society can be happy pagans coasting through a life filled with abundance. Yet they'll always wonder if there isn't something more—another reality. Never satisfied, they hope to fill the void by making one more dollar or conquering one more mountain.

The red pill, by contrast, offers the truth, but promises nothing more. If you do follow Christ, riches may come, but so may poverty. Social acceptance may come, but so may rejection. The red pill simply helps you see things as they really are.

If Christians thought about the red-pill reality of the church purely in business terms (we know the church is not a business, but let's assume it is for the sake of the argument), what product would we say the church offers? We might define Christianity's product features as transcendence, significance, and community. These features sometimes go by labels such as morality, love, grace, compassion, forgiveness, friendship, kindness, help for raising a family, and hope for life beyond the grave.

These answers are true and right, but incomplete. Christianity's great features and name-brand labels must not be confused with the product itself. The actual product of our faith is two vital relationships: with God through his Son Jesus Christ and with fellow humans through the power of the Holy Spirit. Churches facilitate an ongoing, growing relationship with God and a new way of relating to people that makes forgiveness possible and that builds a series of transforming relationships with others.

> **The actual core product of our faith is relationships—with God and with fellow humans.**

OUR CANCER SCARE

As I was working on this chapter, our doctor told my wife Jodi that she might have cancer. It was the first time either of us had personally encountered this dreaded enemy, and we were terrified.

Both of us have the privilege of a vital, personal relationship with God. We trust in God's goodness. We have confidence that he cares for us. We believe that the surprise and shock we felt during this confusing time does not reflect the whole picture of his plans for our lives.

Just before we went to bed after that long day of receiving and pondering the unexpected news, I dashed off a "please pray—we're scared" e-mail to family and friends. When I logged on to the computer the next morning, I found more than forty e-mail replies awaiting us. Every single one had positive words from people who cared and would pray for us during our dark hour. Many people offered specific help, such as watching our children when we went to the hospital the next week for a day of exploratory tests.

When Jodi's biopsy came back as benign, these same people were there to celebrate with us that all was well and that the scare was over. We poured out our hearts to God in gratitude for his physical touch.

Hollywood may pay people $750,000 per episode to act like *Friends* on a hit TV show. In real life, money can't buy what Jodi and I experienced. Our breadth and depth of relationship with these people came not because we all believed in the *Cheers* theme song that says, "Sometimes you want to go where everybody knows your name." Instead, our support emerged through people connected together because of a relationship with God.

WE'RE CERTAINLY NOT IN KANSAS ANYMORE

Relationships are absolutely central to God's purposes. This emphasis begins in the Garden of Eden with Adam and Eve's closeness

> Relationships are absolutely central to God's purposes.

to "the Lord God as he was walking in the garden" (Genesis 3:8). It continued through the creation of the church, with its relationship-driven qualities of unity and oneness as the body of Christ. It will reach its final stage in heaven, when God walks with us again: "Now the dwelling of God is with men, and he will live with them. They will be his people, and God himself will be with them and be their God" (Revelation 21:3).

Relationships are crucial to the Bible's Great Commandments to love (Matthew 22:36-40), its Great Commission to make disciples (Matthew 28:19-20), and its Great Charge for how congregational leaders are to shepherd the church (1 Peter 5:1-4). Every mark of maturity and measurement of health given to the church has a strong relational component (see, for example, Ephesians 4:11-16).

What's new is that today's world has shifted Christianity and the church from the mainstream to the margins of culture. Just as the Matrix replaced the role of human beings, a radical shift has taken place in the way our society sees the church's presence.

The danger is that with all those changes in how churches are engaging society, our core product of relationships has been lost in most people's minds. As we'll discuss later, relationships are the key to reaching the soul of today's generation. Relationships are what Donald McGavran long ago highlighted with the title of his book, *The Bridges of God*.[1] The gospel has for all time and eternity been transmitted in no other way than that of people connecting with other people.

The shift in society's view of the church has resulted in the marginalization of the church and the secularization of society. Christianity has lost its place at the center of American life. (Other resources that discuss these ideas are listed in Appendix D.)

As Christians we can no longer assume that we are the priests, pastors, and moral chaplains of the surrounding community. Instead, our role has been trivialized. Our Matrix-like replacements are a host of value systems that don't depend on God.

> Christianity has lost its place at the center of American life.

The fallout has led an increasing number of people today to feel that religion is a private affair: "You believe what you believe, and I believe what I believe. In this country we have the right to believe as we please, so let's be mutually respectful and not intrude into one another's spiritual views."

Theologians explain that secularization "does not refer to the disappearance of religion from society, but that religion no longer influences society. Religion is distanced from society, relegated to the private lives of its citizens…People see Christianity as having little or no importance in daily life…It does not affect one's moral decisions." [2]

We're Unable to Relate to the Unchurched

On what grounds can I assert to my family or neighbors that I have spiritual insights superior to theirs?

Today it is politically correct to tell someone that drinking while driving could lead to death in an automobile accident, that smoking will likely lead to death from heart disease or lung cancer, and that non-monogamous sex could lead to death from AIDS. But mention that rejecting God leads to death in hell—even with tears of compassion in your eyes—and you invite allegations of harassment, mean-spiritedness, and extremism. Words such as "arrogance," "hate crimes," and "intolerance" can quickly follow.

People today often view Christians unfavorably, and not just because we sometimes make fools of ourselves by still circulating petitions about the irrepressible Madalyn Murray O'Hair-FCC rumor[3] or provide other indicators that we're out of touch. Rather, the major tide of society evidences itself through a host of politically correct replacement values. Recent examples from news headlines include…

- "Bible Makes Christians Intolerant of Jews, Says Boston Globe Columnist"
- "Planned Parenthood Accuses Catholic Church of Waging War Against Women"
- "Canadian Government Agency Bans Dr. Laura Under 'Hate Speech' Laws"

The idea that you are headed to hell unless you trust in Christ for your salvation comes from the Bible (see Matthew 18:7-9; Luke 12:4-10; 2 Peter 2:4-10a; Revelation 20:11-15). But if you use that approach with people today, most of them won't hear what you're saying—they're too busy being offended by their preconceptions. In their minds, the church has no authority in society or in their lives. How dare you try to shove your views down their throat?

Marginalization has become a defining reality for most churches.

This kind of marginalization has become a defining reality for most churches. Until we recognize the extent to which we've been marginalized, we won't know how to respond.

As a result, churches have to figure out a new way to locate their social reality on the current cultural map of North America. Christians must learn how to live the gospel as a distinct people who are no longer at the center of society. We must learn how to build relational bridges that win a hearing.

WE'RE NOT A THREAT; WE'RE IRRELEVANT

In the first century, Christians were seen as a threat. The hand of God was so evident through them that "they were highly regarded by the people" (Acts 5:13). Their lifestyle had huge social repercussions for good wherever they went. The danger was that sometimes their allegiance to God rather than to Caesar was so misunderstood that they were blamed for every imaginable ill of society—people who "have turned the world upside down" (Acts 17:6, KJV).

As Christians in America today, we're not much of a threat to society because we're irrelevant, both to society as a whole and to our next-door neighbors as individuals. The primary reason America is so unchurched is that Christianity has no relevance for the vast majority of those we hope to reach.

STUMBLING BLOCKS ARE MORE CULTURAL THAN THEOLOGICAL

One enormous obstacle facing the church is the damaging perceptions of what Christianity is all about. Why do our secular neighbors find churches to be so irrelevant? Because too often they are. Because we don't have relationships with people to demonstrate otherwise. Because we don't genuinely care enough.

> Our secular neighbors find churches to be irrelevant because we don't have relationships with people to demonstrate otherwise.

The initial stumbling blocks for most unbelievers are not theological, but cultural. The problem that most people have with hearing the gospel is not its teaching about God and his pathway to salvation, but its perceived irrelevance to life today.

This issue of culture and faith is a fundamental one, but I am convinced it isn't understood by most Christians in North America. It seems that people who have experienced cross-cultural missions are the most aware of it. Later we'll devote an entire chapter to the idea of learning to think and live like a missionary.

CLOSE & PERSONAL

Not Satisfied With a Negligible Evangelistic Impact

In the small, central Florida county-seat town of Leesburg, First Baptist Church is a pioneer in the area of taking-it-to-them ministry evangelism. In the past seventeen years, it has grown from a small church of 300 to a church of more than 2,500 people. It consistently ranks in the top one-half of 1 percent of Southern Baptist churches in evangelism.

When senior pastor Charles Roessel arrived in 1976, he was tremendously concerned at the congregation's negligible evangelistic impact. It was unacceptable that First Baptist was on the margins of community life. "I exist for evangelism like a fire exists for burning"—that was the attitude he began to teach people that a Christian must adopt. He urged the congregation to take Matthew 25 to heart, becoming more serious about meeting needs of people in the name of Christ.

The first taking-it-to-them ministry the church launched was hard and not without controversy. It was a rescue mission designed to reach people who were down and out. "Today it's so encouraging to see a guy worth $50 million sitting next to a lady who went through our shelter," says Associate Pastor Art Ayris. But that attitude was not widespread twenty years ago at First Baptist.

According to Ayris, who was on the original steering team for the rescue mission, "The key to our philosophy is to begin right where you are, use what you've got, and begin ministering in that situation. We had a horribly dilapidated old house. We used it to feed and shelter homeless men and families." As church people helped the men, they also refurbished the home.

At the time, Ayris was a lay volunteer. He had come to town as a student in the local college. He began attending church at First Baptist, was baptized there, was married there, got involved teaching Sunday school, became a deacon, began leading outreach, came on staff, and eventually came to head up many of the evangelistic ministries. "We believe in battlefield promotions here," he jokes.

This lay-led, use-what-you've-got rescue mission story is typical of how dozens of ministries have started at First Baptist. For each, the evangelistic linkage is simple and clear: "We meet the need with the hope and intention of sharing Christ," says Ayris.

Eventually the church developed an entire ministry village complex. "Our concept is that people can come to the foot of the cross," explains Ayris. "Whatever their need is, they can come here and receive help, healing, hope, and all of those wonderful things that Christ offers."

Today more than seventy ministries exist, staffed by 1,400 volunteer positions. The ministries range from divorce recovery groups to a crisis pregnancy center. The multiple use of the facilities has caused the church to be known as a seven-days-a-week congregation.

"As we meet needs," summarizes Ayris, "we continually discover people we never would have identified through normal church meetings. You'll find people that you won't find any other way."

That's what First Baptist is all about nowadays. "We are continually seeking new ways to reach people," says Ayris. "We are going to present Jesus Christ to people. People have to see the gospel as well as hear it."

ZERO CULTURAL CONNECTION WITH CHRISTIANITY

One evening after a speaking engagement in Peoria, Illinois, I didn't feel sleepy. I saw a Barnes & Noble bookstore outside my hotel window, so I wandered over, ordered my usual (a grande latte decaf, two sugars, skinny), rambled through the bargain section, and sat down in an armchair to read.

At a table nearby sat six people. I later learned that they were all university students. They were hotly debating a trivia question: What was the skipper's name on *Gilligan's Island*?

As their debate went on, I leaned over and said, "I know."

They all stared at me, waiting for the answer. Here was my moment to find value in all the time I had wasted watching television in junior high. I explained that his full name had appeared only in the pilot and in two other episodes. "Actor Alan Hale played the skipper. His character's name was Jonas Grumby," I said in conclusion, with great pride.

Slack-jawed, they responded, "You must be really old."

I scooted up to their table, and we began talking. They asked me what I did for a living. "I assess, coach, and train entrepreneurs in the nonprofit sector," I explained, a bit covertly referring to my work with people who start new churches. They chatted with me about my life, and I asked them about theirs.

By midnight, I'd discovered that not one of these kids could identify the historical significance of Easter. Two could do Christmas, but the others didn't understand why anyone would celebrate the birth of a "mythical" Jewish carpenter. We continued our conversation until the 2 a.m. closing time. Then we exchanged e-mail addresses and said good night.

As I walked back to my hotel, I kept thinking, "Who's going to reach these people? What voice will they listen to?"

All of them had zero cultural connection with who Jesus is, why churches exist, and what authentic Christians do or believe. They were genuinely clueless about what it means to be real followers of Jesus Christ and what a difference it would make to them.

UNCHURCHED AND UNREACHED, BUT RECEPTIVE

At the same time, the kids were talkative, open, and interested. Imagine the impact Christians could have—if we only knew how to reach people given the realities of today's world.

The young people I met symbolize the challenge of today's church. According to religious pollsters, North America continues to be as religious as ever. The new, significant factor is the increasing number of people who are seeking answers to the basic questions of life *outside*

of churches. This is especially true of young baby boomers and generation Xers. Seminary professor Eddie Gibbs says the latter "represent the
first generation in the history of the United States in which the majority
are beginning their search outside of Christianity, or with a religious
cocktail of their own mixing. The under-35s live with ambiguity and
paradox, able to hold contradictory views at the same time." [4]

So much of the world today is as religious as ever, despite continual predictions during the last two centuries of secularization and that
religion must inevitably decline in the modern world.[5] "What many pun-
dits thought was the death of the church in the 1960s through secularization was really its relocation and rebirth into the rest of the world,"
points out Australian writer Mark Hutchinson in his article about the impact of globalization on the way Christians do ministry.[6]

As these new opportunities unfold, it's time for Christians here on
our home turf to reach the lost in America, rather than appearing to
them that we ourselves are the ones who have lost our way. We need
to do so from a new vantage point, but it can be done.

The cross of Christ must become the emblem of truly selfless people rather than the emblem of practically everything else. It should represent some of the greatest adventures on earth, an invitation to a journey from despair to hope not unlike Morpheus' crusade in *The Matrix*.

RENT THIS MOVIE

Cookie's Fortune
(Comedy/Drama, PG-13)

In a sleepy, intimately small Mississippi town, Jewel Mae "Cookie" Orcutt, who longs for her dead husband, commits suicide. Her sister is the first to find the body. Embarrassed by the suicide, she decides
to fake a murder scene. Good-hearted Willis Richland, the next-door neighbor who had always
helped Cookie around the house, becomes the chief suspect. The tables suddenly turn when some
eye-opening news shows an inherent flaw in the idea of Richland as a suspect.

What to look for: Look at the story through the experience of Willis Richland, the only person who
knows all along that everyone's view of reality is faulty, including that of Cookie's self-righteous sister. If he symbolizes the church and Cookie's sister symbolizes the world, what do you think would
be the most credible way for him to share his secret?

CONNECTIONS

Estimating the Potential Impact in Your Community

Directions: Please check all the statements below that describe spiritual needs in your community, and think of ways you might respond.

Your Community, Starting With You

___ 1. I am not yet certain of my own relationship with God through Jesus Christ, but I would like to be.

___ 2. I have not yet found a church where I feel at home and can grow in my faith, but I would like to find one.

Your Community, Through Your Church

___ 3. I've had very little hope that my church is making any real difference in the community, but I'm willing to try.

___ 4. I have many unchurched friends or relatives who might be open to coming to church with me if I invited them.

___ 5. Other people in our congregation are in the same situation of having friends or relatives who might be open to coming to church with them; I could befriend these new people.

Your Community, Beyond Your Church

___ 6. I don't really know anyone in my community other than the people in my church, but I'm willing to get to know other people.

___ 7. To the best of my knowledge, *my immediate next-door neighbors* don't know much about the power of the gospel to change their lives, but they might be interested.

___ 8. To the best of my knowledge, very few people *on my street or in my housing unit* know firsthand about the power of the gospel to change their lives, but they might be interested.

___ 9. I haven't had much training in how to talk to others about the love of Jesus Christ and the power of the gospel, but I'd like to learn.

___10. I know very little about the many different religious backgrounds represented in my community, but I'm willing to learn if it would help me show others how to become followers of Jesus Christ.

• How many statements did you check? _____

• What percentage of people reading this book do you think could check off at least three of the statements above? _____

• How do you feel after going through this list? Circle the sentence that best matches your thinking:

This country is in big trouble!

The future is full of hope.

We're not doing our part.

God is doing something wonderful.

God is about to do something wonderful.

Attention everyone: It's time to pray!

We've begun to walk our talk.

Other: _____

 ## *Discussion Questions*

1. Why do you think most people do not look to the church for their life's orientation?

2. What single issue do you think makes faith in Jesus Christ unique among world religions or points of view?

3. How is Jesus Christ relevant to your life?

4. How could Christians make Christ's message as relevant as possible today?

5. How can you increase your effectiveness as a witness of Christ's love?

SECTION TWO

CHOICES

CHAPTER 5

How Did Jesus Respond?

Jesus came to earth with one simple mission—to seek and save the lost—which happens only when someone begins a relationship with Christ. He's still seeking and saving the world today by involving willing people like you and me.

BIG IDEA

My wife Jodi and I were out on a date, seated in a theater, watching the James Cameron epic, *Titanic*. I had my arm around her, and we were cuddled in a Hollywood-induced romantic embrace. We had enjoyed the drama and romance. Our hearts had ached as the fictitious hero, Jack Dawson, had given up his life for his sweetheart, Rose, in hopes that she might be one of the few to survive the disaster that had befallen this "unsinkable" ship.

Suddenly, we both chilled at the words Rose voiced as she was reflecting back on that terrible tragedy and describing Jack's heroic action: "Now you all know there was a man named Jack Dawson…and that he *saved me in every way that a person can be saved*. I don't even have a picture of him. He exists now only in my memory."

"Saved in every way?" my mind asked. "Is that what salvation has come to mean to people today?" For Rose, salvation seemed to mean escape through a weeklong, illicit, romantic and sexual interlude. Her Prince Charming named Jack Dawson would free her from a life of entrapment to her selfish, inconsiderate fiancé and from having to take care of her demanding and destitute mother.

While the story was dressed up with all kinds of warm, fuzzy feelings, a magnificent musical score, lavish cinematography, dazzling special effects, and a sweet old woman, it taught a huge sugarcoated lie! The experience Rose described as being "saved in every way" was really the ultimate act of selfishness. Sadly, in the end, salvation to Rose was only getting what she wanted—nothing more, nothing less, and nothing else. She approached her final breath with no clue of the eternal salvation God offers.

In this movie's interpretation, salvation didn't mean coming to terms with one's character (fallen) and behavior (sin). Rather it meant being freed from further obligations. This salvation was empty of any power to forgive Rose's sins, grant her eternal life, or put her in right standing with God. This version of *Titanic* redefined salvation to leave out God and the spiritual.

> **S**alvation to Rose was only getting what she wanted—nothing more, nothing less, and nothing else.

By the way, my point here isn't to trash the movie or James Cameron. If we're going to use the language of the culture to reach people for Christ, it doesn't make much sense to point out everything objectionable in the movie. Good missionaries wouldn't go to another country and knock something in the culture if they were using it to reach people. We start where people are, but we don't continually have to tell them what kind of cesspool surrounds them—we let God show them that. It is foolish to blame darkness for being dark. Our model for this is the Apostle Paul in Acts 17. He didn't ridicule the Greek gods; he said he knew the unknown God for whom they were looking.

Further I, too, have responded to Christ's selfless acts in the way Rose did. I've accepted heaven's offer of salvation, but then I continue living a completely selfish life. Most Christians are guilty of that in some way. From Rose to me, God's salvation has lost its impact.

OTHER PEOPLE WERE REALLY SAVED ON THE TITANIC

The 1997 movie *Titanic* minimized the role Christians played as the ship ultimately took more than 1,500 people to their deaths. Missing from the movie was the Salvation Army Band playing the hymn "Nearer My God to Thee" while many men solemnly sang along as water filled the ship. Gone, too, was the gripping story of a Scotsman named John Harper, a minister of the gospel who was on the Titanic with his six-year-old daughter, Nana. He was traveling to Moody Church in Chicago to preach for three months.

When the alarm bells rang after the ship had struck the iceberg, Harper scrambled to place his daughter in one of the lifeboats. After saying a soul-wrenching farewell to his little girl, he launched his final evangelistic campaign.

As the frigid waters of the North Atlantic filled the doomed passenger liner, Harper is said to have shouted, "Let the women, children, and the unsaved into the lifeboats!" With that, Harper took off his life jacket and gave it to a man nearby. "Don't worry about me," Harper reportedly

(continued)

said, "I'm not going down, I'm going up." Despite the paralyzing cold water, Harper swam to his fellow passengers and pleaded with them to look to Christ as their final moments drew near.

A man Harper had used his dying breath to witness to then turned his life over to Christ. Four years later at a Titanic survivors' meeting in Ontario, Canada, the man tearfully gave his testimony recounting how John Harper had led him to faith in the Lord. Harper had given his life so that the man could be saved in this world and for all of eternity.

According to records originally compiled in 1912 by John Climie and recorded in Moody Adams' book, *The Titanic's Last Hero,* many people came to faith through Harper's efforts during the last moments of his life.[1]

ARE WE THEIR LINK TO JESUS?

More than 1,500 of the 2,200 passengers on the Titanic died when it sank on April 15, 1912. Perhaps the greatest tragedy is that many of those people didn't have to die.

In the book *Red Sky in the Morning,* the authors cite the ideas of evangelist Ron Hutchcraft as they tell the story: "A lot of people climbed into the twenty lifeboats, but many were only half full. Hundreds of people were in the cold water with life preservers. Most of them did not die from drowning; they froze to death. The people in the lifeboats heard the cries of those dying people, but they chose not to go back for fear of capsizing. Only one lifeboat returned—after it was too late. Of the hundreds who were in the water, only six people were rescued. *Those who were already saved didn't go after those who were dying*" [emphasis in original].[2]

Similarly, Christians must reach out to people dying in sin. As Hutchcraft says, "We're surrounded by dying people...We must ask God to break our hearts for those people. We're their link to Jesus."[3]

SAVING REFUGEES

As I consider what salvation has come to mean in today's culture, my thoughts race back to Africa. My responsibility as a new missionary had been to work in a refugee camp in the tiny village of Ka'arachi on the Kenyan-Ethiopian frontier. In those days—the mid-1980s—North Americans couldn't look at a newspaper, magazine, or television news show without being reminded of the tremendous human suffering taking place in the Two-Thirds World.

I'll never forget when the single-engine plane I was riding in touched down on the tiny airstrip. After the plane rolled to a stop, the pilot popped open the fuselage door and the cabin immediately filled with the most horrible stench I'd ever encountered. In a matter of seconds, the pilot led me down the steps, handed me my bag, and said, "I'll have the rest of the team here in two weeks." He turned, taxied, and flew away while I remained in a daze.

I stood there alone on the unpaved airstrip with gritty sand blowing in my face. I began to wonder what I'd gotten into.

I could see the camp of about two hundred acres. It was surrounded by a large berm of dirt and razor wire to keep the bandits and raiders out at night. I had been told that, at times, up to two hundred thousand people would be jammed into it.

After a few minutes, the camp director came walking through the shimmering heat from the direction of the camp. Father Joey, built like a bowling ball, was five feet tall in both directions. Originally from Crete, he had come into a life-changing personal relationship with Jesus Christ during parish ministry in the United States. He had been sent to the desert in hopes of shaking some "sense" into him.

"That's right. I'm in trouble. Praise God!" he said as he finished his short introduction. Then he said, "Let's go to work."

I couldn't wait to begin. I pictured myself putting food in bowls, handing them to people, and saying, "Here, because Jesus is alive, eat."

I pictured myself putting food in bowls and saying, "Here, because Jesus is alive, eat."

But it didn't work out like that. This camp had the capacity to feed only twenty thousand people a day. The math was painful. During peak times, each refugee would get a real meal only once every ten days.

Instead of serving food, I stood in the sun all day with the starving masses, counting to twenty thousand. Finally at the end of the day, I had to push back those who were waiting and close the barbed wire gate. Through tear-drenched sobs, I yelled at those outside, "I'm sorry, you can't eat today."

I entered the staff tent and sat down, joining peers from all over the world. Before us was a simple dinner of rice and protein gravy, an orange, a couple of other items, and a big glass of cold water. It wasn't much, but it was a feast compared to what the refugees had.

I shoved away my food saying, "If they can't eat, I won't eat." The other people around the table were eating, laughing, and sharing. "They're all lunatics," I thought as I stormed out of the staff area and went to the little tent where I was to sleep. "They must be sick or crazy if they can laugh at a time like this."

During the day it was brutally hot, but when the sun went down it became miserably cold. I climbed into a creaky old hammock and stretched the scratchy wool blanket around me, with mosquito netting clinging to my face.

A horrible, ever-present buzzing sound filled the air. People were continually coughing and hacking as their respiratory systems gave way to the final ravages of starvation and malnutrition. Even late into the night, the camp was never quiet.

As I lay in the hammock, I kept thinking, "What am I doing? I've got to get out of here." With hot, angry tears burning across my face, I finally fell asleep.

The next thing I knew, Father Joey's fat hand was grabbing my shoulder. "God wants to talk to you, boy," he said. That was his loving way of saying, "Wake up. Good morning. It's time for our morning prayer meeting."

I thought, "You've got to be kidding." Still in a daze, I followed him through to the staff eating area. The tables had been moved so that people could kneel in prayer. Doctors from Norway and Denmark; nurses from Sweden, Australia, and New Zealand; and aid workers from Brazil, Japan, Canada, and the United States all got on their knees. They asked God for the strength to make it one more day and to really care for the refugees.

My prayer was not very spiritual. I silently said, "God, if you're really there, then get me out of here."

> My prayer was not very spiritual. I silently said, "God, if you're really there, then get me out of here."

BURYING REFUGEES

When we finished praying, Father Joey found me and said, "I have something for you to do. Come with me." As we left the tent, he grabbed an old, dog-eared book and his clerical vestments. As we made our way between the tents, through the razor wire, and over the berm, I saw him kiss the vestments and put them on.

As we reached the crest of the berm, I looked over it and saw something that will forever be etched into my memory. It was a trench about forty feet long, four feet wide, and five feet deep. It was filled from one end to the other with the bodies of little children. I froze in place.

We were going to a funeral! I later learned that two funerals were conducted every day at Ka'arachi—children in the morning and adults at night.

These morning funerals meant far more than saying a painful good-bye to a precious child. We were not only burying these people's children; we were burying their future. What IRAs, Social Security, Medicare, and Medicaid are to people in the United States, children are to many people in East Africa.

Families there try to have many children in hopes that someone will be able to take care of them in their old age. "Old" means in their forties. Life expectancy is about forty-five years because life is so hard. In this region the infant mortality rates are so high that people don't even name their children until the children are three years old.

The trench was surrounded by frail women, some of whom had nursed their babies until their breasts bled in hopes of saving their children. There were virtually no men in the camp. They'd either been conscripted into the army or killed, or they were in hiding trying to wait out the civil war.

I froze in my steps as Father Joey walked to the other end of the trench and opened the book to say things appropriate to those who have lost a loved one. When he got done he told me, "Tom, sing 'The Lord's Prayer.' Go ahead, sing it in English."

I wanted to say, "Sing? Have you lost all of your mind, or just part of it?! Sing?" I wanted to cuss. I wanted to run. I wanted to do anything but sing. I wanted to get as far away from there as possible.

He prompted me again: "Sing." Singing "The Lord's Prayer" in B-flat is tough enough when you're warmed up, but virtually impossible when you're angry, scared, choking on dust, and broken in the heart.

I sang anyway. "Our Father, who art in heaven/hallowed be thy name. Thy kingdom come, thy will be done/on earth as it is in heaven…" My mind checked out at that point. I'm sure I finished the song, but I don't remember much else about that morning.

When I sang, "Thy will be done on earth as it is in heaven," I felt as if I had been hit by a lightning bolt. If ever I could claim that God spoke directly to me, it was in that moment.

BLAMING GOD

As I was singing, the undercurrent of my mind was shouting, "God, how can *you* let this happen?" I will never know how to communicate what that experience did to me. It separated my heart from my head. My head screamed to whatever feelings I had left, "How could a loving God exist if a tragedy like this could remain unstopped?"

I had heard pastors back in the United States confide, "I came to this church to serve you, God, but the way things are going, I'm not even sure if you exist." I had a new appreciation for how they felt.

At that same instant I was questioning God, I believe God was asking me, "Tom, how could *you* let this happen?"

I suddenly understood that for God's will to be done on this earth, I must assume certain responsibilities. My song was voicing God's answer. I am to represent Jesus' kingdom to the people around me. "Jesus said, 'Peace be with you! As the Father has sent me, I am sending you.' And with that he breathed on them and said, 'Receive the Holy Spirit' " (John 20:21-22).

If it's to be, it's up to "Christ in me" (see Colossians 1:27). I have been blessed in order to bless others, an idea found throughout the Bible going back as far as God's covenant with Abra- **I**f it's to be, it's up to me— ham in Genesis 15. God's plan for reaching the **it's up to "Christ in me."** world is to use people—and not just that Chinese missionary many Christians talk about, Brother Ye. ("Go ye, therefore, and teach all nations." See Matthew 28:18-20, KJV.)

All my years of Bible study suddenly became very personal. I realized something about my responsibility in the grand scheme of things that I hadn't previously understood: the importance of personal obedience to the commands of God. As Scripture says, "Whoever claims to live in him must walk as Jesus did" (1 John 2:6).

Not choosing *is* choosing. God is able, through you and me as his vice regents, to accomplish the impossible. Through acts from feeding the hungry to showing genuine compassion to our next-door neighbors, people will know that we are Christians by our love. (See John 13:34-35 and John 15:9-17.)

Many people in those East African camps were saved in every way that a person can be saved. They found food, and their bodies were saved from immediate physical death. They found clothing, and their dignity was saved. They put their spiritual trust in Jesus Christ, and their souls were saved for eternity. They found a purpose in life—people who became Christians eventually ran the camp—which gave them hope that others would also be saved.

All this happened because of the simple, prayerful, loving obedience of Father Joey to Jesus Christ. Because of the chain reaction Father Joey helped start, many Muslims and animists experienced renewal of

body, soul, and spirit. More than Rose Dawson, they were truly saved…
"in every way that a person can be saved."

WHAT IS "GOOD NEWS" TO OUR NEIGHBORS?

The refugees at that camp experienced salvation in a way that many in North America—the vast majority of those we hope to reach—must also be saved. One reason North America has such a large unchurched population is because of the huge gap between what we say and what they need.

North America has such a large unchurched population because of the huge gap between what we say and what they need.

When I was in East Africa, it was easy enough to guess what starving refugees who'd lost everything would receive as good news. Once I returned stateside, however, the challenge was much greater. What was good news to my extended family? What did my church need to be and do in order to show the relevance of Christ to our unchurched, next-door neighbors? What was my responsibility to them as Jesus' follower?

IT ALL BEGINS WITH JESUS

Two thousand years ago, a child was born in an obscure village in a backwater part of the Roman Empire. The boy grew up to be a religious reformer who preached for three years and then was put to death as a nuisance by the Roman colonial authorities. Some observers have interpreted his life as a story of ignoble failure ending in a terrible and shameful death.

In reality, the result of Jesus' public ministry of three years has become the cornerstone of human history. Even a secular publication such as Time magazine affirms: "It would require much exotic calculation, however, to deny that the single most powerful figure—not merely in these two millenniums but in all human history—has been Jesus of Nazareth." Why? Because, the article continues, "a serious argument can be made that no one else's life has proved remotely as powerful and enduring as that of Jesus." [4]

Jesus had three years to lay out his plan to save the world. What did he do? He built a team. He poured his life into building relationships with twelve people, including one who totally failed the training. He involved them in all he did. "Jesus traveled about from one town and village to another, proclaiming the good news of the kingdom of God. The

Twelve were with him" (Luke 8:1). He told them he came to earth "to seek and to save what was lost" (Luke 19:10).

Jesus made it clear that he came with a specific message: "I must preach the good news of the kingdom of God to the other towns also, because that is why I was sent" (Luke 4:43). He then commissioned his disciples to continue his mission after he was gone, promising them the power to do so and saying, " 'As the Father has sent me, I am sending you.' And with that he breathed on them and said, 'Receive the Holy Spirit' " (John 20:21-22).

> "The single most powerful figure—not merely in these two millenniums but in all human history—has been Jesus of Nazareth."—*Reynolds Price* in Time magazine

By word and example, Jesus emphasized that seeking and saving what was lost was a top priority. He trained his disciples to do likewise in the making of new disciples. His mission remains urgent today because Jesus Christ offers the only lasting antidote to the ills that plague our souls and our society.

EVERYTHING IS WRONG BECAUSE OUR PERCEPTION IS WRONG

Both religious and irreligious people look to Jesus as an example and inspiration. Why, then, do our families, neighbors, and friends not see the widespread life transformation that Jesus' ministry heralded? Because we're not focused on what he came to do. Because we sometimes have a too small view of his power in our lives. Because we don't view Jesus as he is.

The truth is that the power of Jesus lives in us to do big things. But our biggest deficiency is that our Jesus is too small. The first-century church didn't view him that way. They didn't put their trust in education, politics, or church-growth techniques. They weren't fat and soft. They also had an understanding of suffering that middle- and upper-class Americans cannot relate to.

We love the benefits of following Christ, but we skip talking about the costs. We proclaim the value, but not the price. Jesus says, "If anyone would come after me, he must deny himself and take up his cross daily and follow me" (Luke 9:23).

> We serve a God who calls and sends. He is not primarily interested in our comfort.

We serve a God who calls and sends. He is not primarily interested in our comfort. He wants us to experience him as he is and then spread that good news to others.

This "little Jesus" pattern is not new. In *Your God Is Too Small,*[5] British author J.B. Phillips built a case for the destructive, unreal God that we create: a resident policeman, a grand old man, or a pale Galilean. He asserted that most people's favorite is God in a box—someone too small and inadequate for us.

But just how big *is* Jesus—the real Jesus? He's bigger than our problems. No one has a problem that is bigger than he is. There's not a sin, disease, or human condition that is bigger than he is. At the same time, he comes right to our level, communicating with us in ways we can understand.

The discovery of how big God is leads to a golden opportunity. Instead of prompting us to send out another small lifeboat, we develop a boldness to lovingly debunk the straw man—the false Jesus—in so many people's minds.

Often when I meet people who recount some terrible experience they've had with religious people, I ask them to describe the Jesus they saw in that person or organization. I then ask, "Is that the Jesus represented by the Bible?" They usually say no. When they throw in the medieval Crusades, I ask the same, and they say no. When they describe the atrocities of Hitler, whose armies had "God with us" imprinted on their belt buckles, I ask the same, and they say no.

Ultimately they sense that it's not the Jesus of the Bible they have trouble with; it's someone else. In an information-overloaded society, where people are confronted with thousands of messages every day, the one thing people must hear, see, touch, or feel is an accurate representation of the real God with an open invitation to meet him.

EVERYTHING ELSE IS WRONG WHEN OUR PERCEPTION IS WRONG

If we have a faulty view of Jesus, we're reluctant to engage people with the gospel because we really don't believe it's sufficient to deliver them from their bondage. If we allow ourselves to respond to the true gospel of Jesus Christ versus our incomplete view, we'd understand what it means to know that *Jesus is God*. We'd be willing to make his priorities our priorities. We'd be willing to let him cleanse the junk from our lives that we enjoy and don't want to give up. We'd be consumed by his desires, such as to seek and save the lost. " 'My food,' said Jesus, 'is to do the will of him who sent me and to finish his work' " (John 4:34). Even in his youth he asked, "Did you not know that I must be about my Father's business?" (Luke 2:49, NKJV).

If I yield to him, then he builds in me the capacity to see people the way he does—with hope. I won't give up on people because Jesus doesn't.

I won't give up on people because Jesus doesn't.

When I'm in relationship with Jesus, I become acutely aware of his plan. His first desire for me is that I fully obey him. "If you love me, you will obey what I command" (John 14:15). The confidence Jesus had in his calling becomes mine. His caring about unwanted, outcast people becomes mine. I find myself growing in compassion, becoming slow to anger and quick to forgive. By the power of the Holy Spirit, I begin to live the truth that "whoever claims to live in him must walk as Jesus did (1 John 2:6). If these things aren't happening, then maybe I haven't encountered the real Jesus of the Bible.

Our churches, in turn, must be safe communities to hear dangerous messages about an authentic relationship with an awesome God. Jesus is willing to be known. Ask him to reveal himself to you. Ask him to show you the stereotypes that you've brought into your understanding of his grace.

Go find him, for he's willing to be found. "God...rewards those who earnestly seek him" (Hebrews 11:6). Ask him to show you how big he is and how he does things "immeasurably more than all we ask or imagine, according to his power that is at work within us" (Ephesians 3:20).

PEOPLE OFTEN SUSPECT SOMETHING BETTER IS UNDERNEATH

People may view the church as irrelevant and as having an agenda that's not necessarily in their best interests, but when they get down to *who Jesus is,* they usually show more interest. The stuff we've made important becomes a barrier and keeps people from hearing what we're trying to say. They know in their hearts that there's hope in the message of Jesus, but we don't give them the message they need to hear.

Once upon a time a preacher provided a children's sermon as a part of his message. One Sunday as all the little kids sat around him, he asked, "I'm thinking about a little animal that runs around in your front yard and has a bushy tail. Does anyone know what it is?" No takers. "It also has buck teeth, it likes to eat nuts, and it jumps from tree to tree. Can anyone guess what I'm talking about?" Still no takers. "Well, it might be

People may view the church as irrelevant, but when they get down to who Jesus is, they usually show more interest.

gray or red or sometimes almost black."

Finally a child in the back said, "Well pastor, I know the answer has gotta be Jesus, but it sure sounds like a squirrel to me."

Too often all we give is a squirrel when people really want Jesus. We have opportunities to give others the real goods, but instead, all they can find in our lives and church services is something small and incapable, something other than the real Savior. When people listen to our message, they hear about the Jesus of our culture rather than the Jesus of the Bible. They hear about a Jesus who has been reduced to a self-help guru or a success icon or an emotional masseur.

In their hearts, most people still believe that there's something special about Jesus. They want to hear that the hopes and the dreams for their lives, as well as the solutions to life's complications, can be found in God. But when they turn to the church, if it looks like a squirrel to them, they'll carry their search elsewhere.

> **The world has the wrong image of what it's like to follow Jesus because God's people have been showing the wrong model.**

What would happen if they saw people whose lives have been changed for good? The world has the wrong image of what it's like to follow Jesus because God's people have been showing the wrong model.

Up Close & Personal

Salem Baptist Church Looks for Ways to Win a Hearing

When James Meeks was a seminary student, he decided to major in telling people about Jesus. "I didn't know how to do evangelism, but I wanted to learn how to win the lost, and then to teach others," he says. He never got to take those classes because, in his first semester, he was called to pastor a 95-year-old church in his hometown on the south side of Chicago.

After five years there, he sensed God's call to start a new church that would be solidly based on his passion for evangelism. "The goal of the church is to seek and save the lost," he explains. "I wanted to develop 'desperate disciples' who are totally unashamed of Jesus and willing to take drastic measures to win the lost."

James and his wife Jamell attracted about two hundred followers to this dream. The new church began meeting in rented facilities. "The key with us in the early days was small victories," he explains. "Each victory helped us believe that God can do something greater." So he led the young congregation through a series of short-term goals—everything from how many doors they knocked on to how many people they reached through their Sunday school. "All you have to have is a goal to double where you are," he says. "The speed of the leader is the speed of the team."

He also kept the church focused on its vision and mission. "Whenever anything pulled him off track, he kept coming back to evangelism," says Jamell.

In all of the church's outreach efforts, the young pastor led the people of the church to do the ministry. Referring to Jesus' feeding of the five thousand he explains, "There would have been a lot of hungry people if they had waited for Jesus to personally give them bread and fish."

Today, more than fifteen years later, Salem Baptist Church runs the largest Sunday school in the city of Chicago. The church also sponsors the largest Christian bookstore in the city, housed in an 11,000-square-foot converted liquor store.

They continue to set outreach goals, but now on a much larger scale. "The only reason people don't know how big God is," he says, "is that they don't see Christians doing God-sized things. So I want to find something no one has done and do it for the glory of God, to show others that it can be done." For example, the church maximizes the impact of the worship services by using five different forms of media: the worship auditorium itself, closed-circuit video overflow, television, radio, and Internet—all live, all simultaneous. Videotapes and audiotapes are available afterward.

In 1999 the church set a goal to win 25,000 people to Christ. The people did everything imaginable to win a hearing for the gospel, such as wearing "Ask Me" buttons so that colleagues at work would inquire, "What am I supposed to ask you?" At that point the Christian would reply, "I want you to ask me how to get to heaven." By late August, Salem Baptist Church had collected more than 26,000 signed decision cards. By year's end, the church had baptized 2,900 people.

"It's important to have a goal," James Meeks says. "Without setting the right goals, we might be a church that majors in everything but evangelism."

LET YOUR RELATIONSHIP WITH GOD BE YOUR GUIDE

Seminary professor and former pastor Terry Wardle, author of *The Soul's Journey Into God's Embrace,* writes, "Christ's love relationship with God the Father was foundational to his ministry. Repeatedly in Scripture we see our Lord getting apart to commune with God. He found places of solitude where he sought the Father's love, direction, and empowerment...Relationship enabled Jesus to work in perfect harmony with the kingdom [of God] and made him effective in service to broken and lost people." [6]

You, too, were made to bask in the presence of God through a daily trust relationship with Jesus Christ. God has made a way for you to experience the wonders of his transforming love. This intimacy with God is the ultimate pursuit of the life of faith. It is not as much a zeal for a cause as it is a daily inner longing for a fresh touch from him.

"If you intend to offer Christ to the world in a way that is meaningful and relevant, you must give time and energy to growing in relationship with him," says Wardle. "Apart from that, only imbalance and spiritual ill health result." [7]

Jesus is alive today, and every Christian has access to his love through the Holy Spirit. Jesus waits to meet you and to empower, enlighten, and care for you. As an outgrowth of that real and life-transforming relationship, you will become a contagious, infectious Christian.

Jesus came to earth with one simple mission—to seek and save the lost—which happens only through a relationship with him. He's still seeking and saving the world today by involving willing people like you and me. How can we rest, sleep, or eat until we've committed to show the true Jesus to our neighbors?

How can we rest, sleep, or eat until we've committed to live Jesus to our neighbors?

YOUR NEXT STEP IS A FAITH WALK

Walking is basically a controlled fall. At each step, there's the potential to plant our faces painfully into the floor. Thirty-nine years ago, I took my first steps. Good thing I was born short.

With every opportunity to trust God, we also have the opportunity to fall through unmet expectations or disappointment. We have no guarantee of success. But each time we do trust, whether it's for something small or large, we add to our skill as a walker. We get better at it. The path may be smooth or bumpy, gently rolling or steep. We may still stumble, shuffle, or occasionally limp. But the longer we walk in faith, the more natural it becomes.

Jesus' impact on us comes in direct proportion to our relationship with him. The more we experience his "great salvation" (Hebrews 2:3), the more we will have a sense of needing to share that good news with others. "For Christ's love compels us, because we are convinced that one died for all, and therefore...those who live should no longer live for themselves but for him (2 Corinthians 5:14-15).

EACH STEP YOU TAKE MAKES A DIFFERENCE

A couple taking a morning stroll along the beach noticed that thousands of starfish had been washed up by the tide and stranded on the beach. With the tide going down and the hot sun rising, the starfish were certain to die.

About a mile into their walk, the couple noticed a young man who was throwing starfish one by one back into the ocean. Aware that the man couldn't possibly get to all of the starfish in time, they called out to him, "You have miles to go. What you're doing can't possibly matter."

Holding up a starfish he replied, "It matters to this one," and tossed it back into the life-refreshing sea. "And this one," he said as he saved another. Then he bent down to pick up yet another one.

We've all heard the story about the man and the starfish, and we know that small things can add up to make a big difference. As George Barna notes, "If the total unchurched population were to be decreased by just one percentage point...that would bring an additional two million adults into Christian churches. To put that in perspective, if those two million newcomers were divided evenly among all of the Protestant and Catholic churches in America, each congregation would grow by six people. That's more growth than the average congregation has seen in a long time." [8]

RENT THIS MOVIE

Casablanca
(Drama/Romance, PG)

In 1941, Casablanca is a last refuge for scoundrels. They gather at Rick's Café Americain, where proprietor Rick Blaine receives a pair of stolen exit visas. Should he use them for himself and a former lover, or will he give both visas away? At first he says, "I stick my neck out for nobody." As the movie unfolds, he risks everything for complete strangers. It ends with the individualist giving up even his future isolation, concluding, "I think this is the beginning of a beautiful friendship."

What to look for: In the movie, sooner or later everyone ends up at Rick's Café. Why is that true? In what ways was Rick Blaine like Jesus Christ in the sense that Jesus' most durable impact came through relationships? Compare Rick's response to his dilemma with your church's and your current situation.

CONNECTIONS

Learning to Tell Your Story

Get together with a good friend and complete each of the four statements below. Try to develop a clear, concise comment for each one. Then talk about what you could do to make your story flow more naturally.

1. Before I had a faith relationship with Jesus, my life was...

2. Jesus became real to me when...

3. Since I met Jesus my life is...

4. _____ says that you can know him too. (Insert a quote from the Bible, such as one of those listed in Appendix C.)

Discussion Questions

1. Do people have a harder time relating to Jesus or to Christians? Why?

2. Why do you think so many people find it uncomfortable to talk to friends about Jesus Christ?

3. Describe a time you wished you could have talked about your faith in Jesus.

4. What do you think is the best way to approach lost people about the good news of God's love through Jesus?

CHAPTER 6

WHAT COULD EVERY CHURCH DO?

My church's neighborhood is a mission field. Your church's neighborhood is, too. Does your church live as if that's true?

BIG IDEA

During the Civil War, one of the infantry regiments from Maine decides to go back to the comforts of home. They are tough, battle-hardened veterans who have done their duty. They believe they have the right to return home since their regiment has been recalled, even though their individual enlistments don't expire for another year.

Maj. Gen. George Meade doesn't see it that way. He labels it a mutiny, arrests the men, and hands them over to Col. Joshua Lawrence Chamberlain with the words, "Get them to fight or shoot them." Meade believes the mutineers should join the infantry regiment that Chamberlain leads since it's also from Maine. Reluctantly, Chamberlain accepts.

The movie *Gettysburg* depicts the speech Chamberlain makes to persuade the rebellious troops to rejoin the battle.

"I've been talking with Private Bucklin and he's told me about your problem," Chamberlain begins. "I've been ordered to take you men with me."

"Here's the situation," he explains. "The whole Reb army is up that road a ways waiting for us…We could surely use you fellas. We're now well below half strength. Whether you fight or not that's, that's up to you. Whether you come along—well you're comin'."

"All of us volunteered to fight for the Union just as you did," he continues. "Some came mainly because we were bored at home [and] thought that this looked like it might be fun. Some came because we were ashamed not to. Many of us came because it was the right thing to do. All of us have seen men die."

Chamberlain's words now turn a corner that catch the men by surprise. "This is a different kind of army. If you look back through history you will see men fighting for pay, for women, or for some other kind of loot; they fight for land, power, because a king leads them, or just because they like killing. But we are here for something new. This has not happened much in the history of the world."

At this point he delivers the heart of his sermon: "We are an army out to set other men free...It's the idea that we all have value, you and me. What we're fighting for...in the end...we're fighting for each other."

A long silence ensues.

"You go ahead, you talk for a while. If you choose to join us, if you want your muskets back, you can have 'em...Gentlemen, I think if we lose this fight we lose the war."

Onward they go, together, to win the most decisive battle of the war.

AN ARMY OF FOREIGNERS?

Today another kind of fight for freedom is taking place all around us. It's a mission to give people the freedom to spend eternity in the joyful presence of God. It's a situation in which many of the troops have decided to wear their uniforms, while also insisting that they'd prefer not to do any more battle. It's something that came alive to me while I was wearing my road-warrior uniform.

Picture me standing in line at the Holiday Inn near New York's JFK airport. I strike up a conversation with the three men standing behind me. By accent and appearance they seem to be African, perhaps Nigerian (which they later confirm).

"First time to the States?" I ask.

They indicate yes.

"Hey, welcome!" I continue. "What brings you here?"

They say that they're here for a training conference.

"What line of work?" I ask.

They tell me that they're Christian ministers.

"Great! What's the conference all about?" I ask.

They say that it's a foreign missions field orientation.

"Missionaries—great! To where?" I probe.

I'm caught a bit off-guard when they indicate that their destination is the United States. One of the three explains: "He's going to Los Angeles, he's going to Chicago, and I'm staying here in New York."

Then I think I have it figured out. "What a vision," I say. "Coming all this way to reach expatriated Africans with the gospel! Praise God."

That's not what they have in mind. "Well, sir," one of them explains, "our prayer is to reach anyone we can with the light and love of Jesus Christ."

They'd attended a missionary conference at their church in Nigeria. Their Nigerian pastor, after showing slides depicting life in *American* urban centers, had pleaded, "Who will go to take the gospel to this dark land?"

Their Nigerian pastor, after showing slides depicting life in *American* urban centers, had pleaded, "Who will go to take the gospel to this dark land?"

What irony. Things have come full circle. Christians used to refer to Africa as the dark continent. Now, despite the fact that we're the information capital of the world, the United States is in darkness. Americans tend to think of ourselves as the world's primary sending nation. Now other nations are sending missionaries to help *us*: "Other Christians around the world send, collectively, more missionaries to the United States than are received by any other country in the world except Brazil."[1] Indeed, as noted in an article in Christianity Today, "Nearly as many missionaries are being sent out from Two-Thirds World countries as are being sent to them."[2]

My encounter with the three zealous Christians was humbling. They significantly challenged my perspective.

Church consultant Kennon Callahan warned a decade ago that "the day of the churched culture is over. The day of the mission field has come."[3] Today the situation is even more dire. We no longer need just pastors who think like missionaries; now the *entire congregation* needs to be deputized like church staff. To recast Callahan's statement: The day of the church *member* is over. The day of the church *minister* has come.

The day of the church *member* is over. The day of the church *minister* has come.

As Christians, we need to change our mindset from parishioners to participants, from consumers to contributors, from my congregation to our community, and from "bring them in" to "be among them." A mission outpost view of the local church helps turn a landmark into a lighthouse. It increases a church's ability to offer acceptance and hope to our unchurched family members, neighbors, and friends.

If Christians begin to think like missionaries, our churches will have to behave in new ways. It starts with a willingness to put on our waders and walk out into the stream of our society, showing the world the relevancy of Jesus Christ.

It starts with a willingness to put on our waders and walk out into the stream of our society.

CLOSE & PERSONAL

Phoenix Church Views Itself As a Mission Outpost

Walt Kallestad felt like a complete failure at the end of his first year as a pastor. The relatively young church was in debt, deeply divided, desperately confused, declining in attendance, and depleted of hope. People were already calling loudly for his resignation.

Yet Kallestad had come from Minnesota to northwest Phoenix with a dream. He continued to sense that God wanted it to become reality. "I wanted more than anything else to establish that dream at Community Church of Joy," he says.

"Our primary vision that first year was survival," Kallestad says of his fateful 1979 experience. None of the members seemed to believe that they should reach out beyond their own membership. "Though only a few years old, we'd moved very quickly from being a mission to being a maintenance organization," he remembers.

Through a series of defining moments, Kallestad created a personal mission statement. It included a resolve to lead the congregation from an inward to an outward focus. "When I defined myself, everything changed," he says. "I imagined a congregation that would grow to a point where it could be a powerful witness to Jesus Christ all over the northwest corner of Phoenix. I began with the vision and focused my energy in that direction. I became vision-centered rather than problem-centered."

The next step was to find other leaders to share in creating and developing that vision. "We needed a clear and inspiring vision that would pull us toward the future," Kallestad explains. He enlisted fellow "imagineers" and got together with them on a leadership retreat. "We needed a missionary spirit and a zeal for others at the very heart of our vision."

That's exactly what happened. Kallestad says, "God gave us a vision to say to all people in northwest Phoenix who belonged to no church, 'Come with us.' "

The vision began to catch and spread, and a compelling sense of mission soon began to emerge. It gave people a decisive opportunity to sign on or sign off. Enough people said yes that momentum continued to grow. Over the next two decades, some 70 percent of the new people coming to Joy could be described as unchurched. Today, with more than three thousand people in worship each weekend, the church has become a role model and teaching center for thousands of other congregations that have made similar transitions.[4]

CULTURE IS NOT THE ENEMY

Jesus teaches the idea that "If a man owns a hundred sheep, and one of them wanders away, will he not leave the ninety-nine on the hills and go to look for the one that wandered off?" (Matthew 18:12). But many churches have replaced the image of the seeking shepherd with one of Little Bo-Peep. The nursery rhyme character has also lost her sheep and doesn't know where to find them. Her solution is to leave them alone and they'll come home. The problem is that people are no longer finding their way back to church. Jesus' model is for us to get off our tails and find them.[5]

Ask God to protect you as you enter the stream and then get out there. Jesus talked about living water to a woman at a public well, made spiritual analogies about financial investments when eating at a tax collector's home, and introduced the idea of fishing for men as he hung out at a fishermen's workplace. He used agrarian terms with farmers, religious references with synagogue scholars, and banking concepts with wealthy people. Jesus acknowledged the language and demeanor of the culture and started there. He modeled how to be *in* the world but not *of* it.

> Jesus acknowledged the language and demeanor of the culture and started there. He modeled how to be in the world but not of it.

Jesus didn't teach his followers to join their culture in ways that would disappoint God—for example, by having sex out of marriage because that's what everyone else does or by looking out for "number one" because that's how everyone else seems to live.

Nor did he treat human society as something beyond the scope of his love, or as something right-living people can't influence for fear that the evils of society will overpower them. Following Jesus' example, it would be wrong to view culture as the enemy because "in reality, *such a viewpoint inevitably sees real people as the enemy*"[6] [emphasis in original].

> "Don't compromise the gospel by *not* allowing it to be relevant to contemporary culture."—*Randy Rowland*

Randy Rowland is the pastor of Church at the Center in Seattle, Washington. He explains the balance like this: "Don't compromise the gospel for the sake of popular culture. At the same time, don't compromise the gospel by *not* allowing it to be relevant to contemporary culture…To accommodate the culture by selling out the gospel is to lose all content. To be irrelevant to culture is to hide our light under a basket."[7]

The more significant issue is that too many Christians have essentially no friendships outside the church's membership that go beyond the level of "What's new?" or "How are the children?" And churches rarely behave in ways that make newcomers feel wanted—despite the fact that their signs say "everyone welcome." The net result is that most Christians today are surrounded by people that their church is *presently* incapable of reaching.

> **Most Christians today are surrounded by people that their church is *presently* incapable of reaching.**

Researcher Kent Hunter says: "Our research shows that most Christians don't have a clue to what the mission of the church is…up to 80 percent of church members believe that the primary purpose of the church is to provide a place of fellowship where Christians can share God's love with one another rather than reach out to those who are unchurched."[8]

HOW TO BE USED BY GOD

1. Start where you are, with family and with friends whom you already know.

2. Be yourself with them. Don't think you have to be like anyone else to be effective in helping people discover the love of Jesus.

3. Include them in *your* interests and hobbies, building and deepening your relationships in the process. You are more "alive" when you're doing things you like to do.

4. Do other things together, cultivating intentional friendships with those who haven't yet experienced the personal love and forgiveness of God through Jesus Christ.

5. Pray for those people regularly by name, and look for their needs in terms of transcendence, significance, and community.

6. Find a way to genuinely serve them. Reach them through their hearts more than through their heads.

7. Be especially prayerful and available when they face tough times, knowing that as people face crises they often turn to balanced, spiritually centered, trusted friends.

8. Respond with "I care" statements and actions. Make sure your actions speak louder than your words. *(continued)*

9. Ask leading questions rather than telling them answers. Remember that most people prefer to discover the truth themselves.

10. Invite them to make a step toward God. Ask them what God is teaching them. Ask them how they would like you to pray for them.

I teach a workshop called "Seven Habits of a Visitor-Friendly Church" (see Appendix D), and after interviewing seminar participants from hundreds of churches, I'm convinced that the vast majority of veteran church-goers have not made the uncomfortable changes necessary to be ready for guests. This is true whether the church ranks evangelism as third priority, second priority, or even top priority.

Research shows that "nine out of ten pastors call their church 'evangelistic.' However, less than one out of three church attenders has shared his or her faith in Christ with a non-Christian within the past twelve months." [9] Something is desperately wrong with this picture!

> The need is for a change in outlook and behavior to a model based on a relational concept of evangelism—one that centers on the most fruitful ways of impacting friends, neighbors, and family today.

What has to be done and how can we do it? The need is for a change in outlook and behavior to a model based on a relational concept of evangelism—one that centers on the most fruitful ways of impacting friends, neighbors, and family today.

YOUR MISSION BEGINS JUST OUTSIDE YOUR DOOR

Last spring Jodi and I held a garage sale at our home. As I struck up conversations with guests, I conducted a little survey. "Where's your accent from?" I asked everyone who didn't seem to be born locally. I tallied twenty-one nations, with people representing all social classes from a physician to an unskilled laborer. Pointing this out to Jodi, we also noted that within a few blocks of our home are Vietnamese, Thai-Dam, Korean, Bosnian, Mexican, and Asian Indian restaurants. There is also a large and growing international student community.

As inconsequential as Des Moines, Iowa, might seem to some, the world was here at my doorstep.

When I visit Warren and Michelle Bird, who live just outside of New York City, I feel like I'm at a huge United Nations tea party. You can find whatever group of people God has called you to reach. Cultural distance there is measured in blocks or miles, and not in oceans, time zones, or national borders.

Even in the vanilla-looking heartland of America, Jodi and I can find countless outreach opportunities. The same is true with the world around your church—no matter where you're based—if you'll just open your eyes. The world is as big as six billion people and as small as your neighborhood. The invitation of *Lost in America* is from my "two kids, a minivan, and a dog" suburb of Des Moines to the community that you have unique access to. Your world of opportunity is close by, wherever you live.

> The world is as big as six billion people and as small as your neighborhood.

Warren Bird was in a planning meeting with leaders from his church in Princeton, New Jersey. "How many of you are concerned that not all the members of your immediate family will be with you in heaven?" he asked. Many hands went up. "Now think of the households to the immediate left and right of your front door," he continued. "Is there anyone who has built strong enough relationships to ask about the spiritual well-being of both homes?" One hand went up. "It's taken us years," that person commented, "I've partnered with a Christian neighbor who lives fifteen houses away. We've held barbecues to get to know our neighbors, we've done Bible studies with some, and we've been intentional about inviting people to church. Three of the homes have had someone come to faith in Christ, and they're all now active in a church."

Imagine the world impact if every church took more seriously Jesus' words about being his witness through the power of the Holy Spirit both locally and cross-culturally—and "to the ends of the earth" (Acts 1:8).

Faithful, reproducing local churches have the capacity to bring closure to the Great Commission in just one generation by beginning their mission right here, in addition to entering into cultures overseas.

> Faithful, reproducing local churches have the capacity to bring closure to the Great Commission in just one generation.

WHAT ARE PEOPLE ACTUALLY HEARING?

We must start in the same place that we would if we were brand new missionaries to our neighborhood. We'd begin in prayer and then ask, "What would be the good news to these people?" Look for interest and needs in the areas of transcendence, significance, and community (see Chapter 3).

Missionaries speak of exegeting their culture. We must likewise ask a lot of questions, seek answers, test what we think we've learned, and then ask a lot more questions.

Imagine that you're a missionary who goes to another country. After prayer, what's the first thing you will do? Learn the language and culture—how to communicate in ways that people can hear. In the same way, you need to be aware of and use the cultural language not only of North America in general, but also of the specific people that God is calling you to build bridges toward.

For example, have you noticed these general trends in today's postmodern culture? Randy Rowland calls them "the three no's":

• No certainty—Every truth claim is up for grabs.

• No closure—Salvation is seen as a process or a journey, not an end point or a starting point. It's a marker on the highway.

• No control—We don't have much control over our lives and our world.[10]

HOW DOES YOUR CONGREGATION BECOME A CONTAGIOUS WITNESS?

1. Add to your standard curriculum new information and results of studies about how to effectively reach out to others.

2. As a congregation, prioritize outreach, evangelism, faith sharing, and faith nurturing as important reasons for your existence as a church.

3. Become more intentionally "a house of prayer." Seek God's guidance and petition God for family members and friends who you desire to find new hope and life through Christ.

4. Remember that the way you love is the mark of your witness.

5. Seek out and invite into your fellowship people who don't have a Christian family heritage or a church home.

6. Make changes if necessary so that newcomers feel welcome and wanted.[11]

One way of responding to these realities is found in churches that are reaching our postmodern world. They start with a story instead of Scripture. If you start with someone's faith story, people will accept it as that person's truth. Then, pointing out that it's based on the Bible leads people one step closer to believing that Scripture is true.

Since our country is home to so many religions now, we also need to learn how to reach people who grew up speaking other faith languages.

For example, Buddhists have similar terminology to Christianity—but with totally different meanings—from baptism to being born anew. We can't use the same terms that we always have and expect people from other faiths to respond. They will merely think we are agreeing with them as they interpret our conversation with their own definitions.

As you exegete your surrounding neighborhood, the most important activity, after prayer, is to listen. Significantly, the two highest conversion-growth churches in U.S. history, Saddleback Community Church in the greater Los Angeles area and Willow Creek Community Church in greater Chicago, both begin their stories by saying that they took a survey. The leaders of those churches didn't presume to know what would be good news to people.[12]

After we've gotten a small handle on what the culture around us is looking for, we then ask the more telling and difficult question: How can we show that Jesus is the answer—how can we *become* the good news to these people? What should our church be up to, about, and into if God were really with us in this community? Take off the gloves, dream big, and be creative about how to seek justice, love mercy, and walk humbly with our God in your community.

According to the findings of a professionally developed survey of ten thousand people that I helped conduct for some new church starts in Princess Anne County, Virginia, there are four basic reasons why almost two hundred million people in North America will not be in church this weekend:

1. They view the church as irrelevant.

2. They've never been invited. Some people thought that they had to be a member before they could even visit or that they needed a sponsor as they would at a country club.

3. They have the mistaken notion that churches care more about their money than about them.

4. They've said yes to Jesus, but no to the church (they are "church damaged"). They have endured some horrible experience in a previous church and, therefore, they are angry at God and feeling hurt, let down, or betrayed.

While churches may state that they're in the evangelism business, performance and perception indicate anything but. Many unchurched people believe the church is only after their money.

IF YOU DON'T KNOW WHERE YOU'RE GOING, YOU'LL END UP SOMEWHERE ELSE

Your church can overcome each of these four factors with the people in your community. One way to start is by asking two simple questions. The first is "What business are you in?" Churches can be involved in a lot of different businesses. They can participate in the soul-winning, disciple-making business. Others are in the banking and real estate business. Some churches are in the business-as-usual business.

The second question is "How's business?" Consider what your outcomes are and how you measure if you're succeeding or not. Jesus met the three needs we introduced in Chapter 3. How do you measure your level of fruitfulness?

Whether we like it or not, every church's neighborhood is a mission field. One day there will be a reckoning on behalf of the people who live in that mission field. God will decide whether we took this notion seriously or not. Decide today to view your neighborhood or your social network as a mission field and to live as a missionary. You'll never regret that you did.

RENT THIS MOVIE

Saving Private Ryan
(Drama/War, R)

Veterans of D-Day affirm that *Saving Private Ryan* achieves a level of realism never before seen in a film. Into this bloody, terror-filled world comes an English teacher, Capt. John Miller. He is given the mission of finding Pvt. James Ryan, whose three brothers were all recently killed in combat. No one is quite sure of Ryan's location. Miller gathers a small group of men to look for a needle in a pile of needles.

What to look for: How does your church's missionary heart compare to Capt. Miller's deeply felt sense of mission? Who is your "Private Ryan"? Who are your church's "Private Ryans"? Describe their condition: How are they behind enemy lines? How are they prisoners of the enemy? What are you willing to endure to get them out?

CONNECTIONS

God's Unique Assignment for You

Of the six billion people on the planet Earth, chances are that your comments to the following statements will be one of a kind. The intent is to help identify the unique ways in which you can reach out to others.

1. Identify an interest, a hobby, or a spare-time vocation that you can do with one or more people.

2. How can you be more intentional about doing this activity with people who may not have a vital, life-transforming relationship with Jesus Christ?

3. How often are you willing to pray for the power to be a practical example of God's love to specific individuals?

4. Will you intentionally serve those people as God shows you needs that you could help them meet?

5. Will you commit to looking for an opportunity, and be willing to seize it, to talk with those individuals about their spiritual interests and needs?

Discussion Questions

1. How has the neighborhood around your church changed in the past thirty years? How have these changes affected your church's ability to minister to the neighborhood?

2. How has the world in general changed? How have these changes affected your church's ability to maintain a vital ministry?

3. How has your church changed on the "inside" in the past thirty years? Have these changes affected its ability to minister?

4. How does the idea of living as a missionary, right where you already live, make you feel?

5. Describe a time you were able to step out of your own culture. How did you feel? What did this experience do for you?

6. How can you increase in your capacity as a missionary right here?

CHAPTER 7

WHAT AM I TO BE?

Don't reduce evangelism to programs or duty, or it will become dead.

BIG IDEA

oward the end of the movie *Schindler's List*, Oskar Schindler physically collapses as he wrestles with the idea that he could have done more to save oppressed Jews from the Nazi regime's death camps. The moment occurs as Schindler and his wife walk toward the car, and Rabbi Levartov hands him some papers.

"We've written a letter trying to explain things," Levartov says. "In case you're captured. Every worker has signed it."

Schindler looks at a long list of signatures below the typewritten text. "Thank you," he says.

His longtime assistant, Itzhak Stern, then places a gold ring in Schindler's hand. Schindler notices an inscription on the ring.

"It's Hebrew," explains Stern. "It says, 'Whoever saves one life, saves the world.' "

Schindler puts the ring onto his finger, nods his thanks, and then begins to talk to himself: "I could've got more…if I'd just…I don't know, if I'd just…I could've got more."

Stern cuts in, "Oskar, there are twelve hundred people who are alive because of you. Look at them."

Schindler continues his lament, "If I'd made more money…I threw away so much money, you have no idea. If I'd just…"

Stern again interjects, "There will be generations because of what you did."

"I didn't do enough," says Schindler.

Schindler starts to lose control, with tears coming; Stern too.

"This car," Schindler continues. "Goeth would've bought this car. Why did I keep the car? Ten people, right there. Ten more I could've got."

Looking around he continues. "This pin." He rips the elaborate swastika from his lapel and says, "Two people. This is gold. Two more people. He would've given me two for it. At least one. He would've given me one. One more…I could've gotten one more person, but I didn't."

Schindler breaks down, weeping. Eventually Schindler and his wife Emilie get into the car and drive away.

THE HUMAN TOUCH

I, too, have had the experience of realizing that my life has made a life-or-death difference to others.

When we were first married, Jodi and I lived in Rockford, Illinois, and shared a four-unit apartment with three other young couples. We got to know the others quite well, especially the guys.

"Hey, what's up?"

"I'm doing the laundry."

"Liar! You had a fight with your wife and you're in the doghouse."

"Yeah?"

"We heard you through the walls. Now do you want to guess why I'm out here, too?" It was a significant bonding time for us guys.

Our downstairs neighbors, Keith and Christiane, were active Mormons. She had grown up in that faith. He had Christian roots, but had converted to the Mormon religion when they were dating.

We had a shared big-investment friendship with Keith and Christiane. We regularly ate pizza as one big family, we shopped for Christmas trees together, and our wives even prepared their Sunday school lessons together.

We had a lot in common. Keith and I came from loud, boisterous families where the importance of an issue was based on the decibel level at which it was discussed. We both discovered that our respective wives came from families where their parents never had arguments in their presence. My first disagreement with Jodi just about devastated her. I couldn't understand what was wrong—all I was doing was making my point. Keith and I helped each other figure out our wives.

Keith and Christiane were far more interested in how we lived than in what we had to say. They wanted to know about the struggles in our marriage. We talked as couples about how we handled money, time, intimacy, and other adjustments.

They came to church with us half a dozen times to special events. But in conversation, religion was a bit off-limits or at least awkward—even on our special pizza nights.

Jodi and I tried using the "Four Spiritual Laws" tract and the helpful

dialogues of Evangelism Explosion. We watched the *Jesus* video together with them. We must have tried a dozen other programmatic resources to help them become authentic and devoted followers of Jesus
Christ, and we prayed all along. Nothing connected.

A year and a half later, Keith and Christiane were helping us pack
our boxes to relocate to another city. On the night before we moved,
Keith said to me, "Would you explain it to me one more time?"

I was so shocked that I asked him why he was interested.

"I've seen how you live, and I want that, too," he said. None of the
programs made the connection as much as how we lived. What we said
had credibility because of how we delivered it.

At the time, I viewed evangelism primarily in a
program mode, both personally and through the
church. I lived as if humanity's basic problem was a
lack of information. If I could help people understand, then they'd certainly turn away from their sins and receive salvation through the Lord Jesus Christ. Jesus had become my managing partner and chief operating officer, and my prime project in life was to give others whatever information
they needed to make the same decisions. All I had to do was tell 'em!

> None of the programs made the connection as much as how we lived.

But I'd learned a better way from Keith. His responses confirmed
that no one wants to be your project, but many
people are open to being your friends.

We didn't realize it at the time, but it was our
friendship that led us to discover what Keith saw
as good news: He could find his life's potential through Christ without
having to fit into anyone else's mold. Somehow he picked up that idea
from me, along with the idea that the Jesus of the Bible offered it to
him—even if his and Christiane's previous experiences with constrictive,
authoritarian religion did not allow that freedom.

> No one wants to be your project, but many people are open to being your friends.

That's what we talked about as I packed. That was the bridge he
needed.

The Holy Spirit used our friendship to show us the key to Keith's
heart which allowed us to share the good news and explain to him how
to have a personal faith in Jesus Christ. We never did have the same
breakthrough with Christiane. But from that point forward, Jodi and I
have wanted our loudest sermon to be our marriage.

By the way, I'm not slighting the role of training, but rather, pointing out my wrong-headed thinking that assumed a program can short-
circuit the need for relationships. In fact, churches that train their people

in how to do personal evangelism are consistently the churches that actually do the most evangelism. Evangelistic activity is directly related to positive church health and growth.[1]

What's the common response when one person tries to explain a religious belief to someone else? According to research, 42 percent of people find it "usually annoying." [2] The annoyance problem does

Churches that train their people in how to do personal evangelism are consistently the churches that actually do the most evangelism.

not typically stem from the gospel itself, which is tremendous news. Rather we simply haven't built the relational context for being welcomed into what many individuals consider a most private area of their lives.

CLOSE&PERSONAL

Church Teaches Its People That "You've Got a Story to Tell"

Bill Bohline feels like he grew up in a church, since his mother was the parish secretary at their family's church. While spending so much time with churchgoers, he observed that most of them didn't know where they were going spiritually. "No one told them there was more—that they could be Spirit-filled or have an ongoing relationship with Jesus Christ," he says.

Today Bohline leads a church named Hosanna! Lutheran just outside of Minneapolis, Minnesota. Its target audience is people just like that—people who are "spiritually lukewarm or comatose." Even the church's purpose statement emphasizes the idea of helping people be intentional and grow in their Christian life: "We of Hosanna! invite you into a lifelong journey with Jesus Christ which leads to a new community and a changed life."

Everything about the church focuses on that journey. "Hosanna! is built on a three-legged stool," says Bohline. "We enter the presence of God as an entire community of faith through worship, we develop closeness and friendships through the 'little church' atmosphere of small groups, and we travel a lifelong path of discipleship that we call the Hosanna! Highway." The various classes and workshops that make up the Hosanna! Highway are designed to "affirm you wherever you are and show you what might be the next step for you."

Bohline started the church in 1980 by knocking on some 1,200 doors. The response has been nothing short of overwhelming which has earned the congregation the nickname "world's fastest-growing Lutheran church" for several years. Everything has mushroomed over recent years, from confirmations (100 in 1991 and 600 in 2000) to worship attendance (550 in 1991 and almost 3,000 in 2000).

"The growing edge for us," Bohline summarizes, "is to encourage our people that 'You have a story to tell.' " In numerous ways, from specialized Hosanna! Highway classes to national programs like the Alpha course, Hosanna! Lutheran trains its people to take the next step in their journey, which includes talking to others. "Telling our story is hard for us Lutherans, who tend to be more passive," he explains. "As Christians we are called to believe, belong, and become more like Christ." Referring to Ephesians 4:13, he says, "Maturing in the faith doesn't just happen. We need to know how to grow."

God First Cared About Us

The good news is that the Creator of the universe reached down to each of us through Jesus Christ, making it possible for our broken relationships with God to be restored. That's the gospel in a nutshell: You and I can have peace with God. We can be "at one" in relationship with him through Jesus Christ, who was God in the flesh.

The Bible says, "We love because he first loved us" (1 John 4:19). When God's love genuinely grabs us, we develop a powerful desire to invite others to share the same experience. "I can't help but love and serve them," you find yourself saying.

"Evangelism begins with God, not with us," affirms Ron Crandall in *The Contagious Witness*. "It begins with God's own nature and with God's activity. Any of us who dare to speak of the God who has met us and who can meet others are only able to do so because this is who God is and what God does." [3]

As Bill Bright, founder of a ministry that has presented the gospel to more than four billion people says, "Our role is to tell everyone who will listen about Jesus...We do this from hearts filled with joy and excitement about our Lord Jesus Christ and with compassion for the lost." [4]

That was Jesus' model: "When he saw the crowds, he had compassion on them" (Matthew 9:36). He met their needs by "teaching...preaching the good news of the kingdom and healing every disease and sickness" (Matthew 9:35).

GOD DOES THE CONVERSIONS

No human has the power to convert another person, but we do have a role as God's instruments. Only God can change the heart of a human being. Only the Holy Spirit can reveal truth to someone, creating a "new person." The Bible describes our role as that of a representative of reconciliation: "All this comes from the God who settled the relationship between us and him, and then called us to settle our relationships with each other...God has given us the task of telling everyone what he is doing. We're Christ's representatives...We're speaking for Christ himself now: Become friends with God; he's already a friend with you" (2 Corinthians 5:17-20, *The Message*).

> No human has the power to convert another person, but we do have a role as God's instruments.

We do our part and leave the results to God. We don't convert people—the Holy Spirit does. "No one can come to me unless the Father who sent me draws him," Jesus says in John 6:44. "Flesh gives birth to flesh, but the Spirit gives birth to spirit" (John 3:6).

God's presence is divine love and the medicine of life. It's wonderful medicine, like no other. We become "contagious carriers of this good infection," says Crandall.[5] We want everyone to "taste and see" what wondrous gifts the Father has bestowed upon us. We are a full-body perfume or fragrance of the love of God in Jesus Christ spread by the Holy Spirit, as Paul says in 2 Corinthians 2:16.

Wounded people tend to wound other people. Rejected people tend to reject people. Abused people tend to abuse people. And people who have been hurt tend to hurt other people.

Likewise, redeemed people want to see others experience the wonders of a positive transformation by God. Fully functional, fully alive, fully forgiven people just can't keep from wanting this for others.

START BY BUILDING INTENTIONAL RELATIONSHIPS

A church's greatest attention-getter is the "I care" personal relationship that addresses a person's needs and interests in a relevant way. This idea certainly has historical precedence. From the practice of Jesus and the early church to the research findings of today's "church growth" and "church health" movements, many people first warm to the gospel when someone meets their needs and builds a relationship.

Many effective Christians have learned how to be more intentional about building personal relationships. Then they bring their friends into the larger faith community either through the front door of a worship service or through the side door of a small group, such as a Bible study or activity group.

This relational pathway isn't the only way to get the job done, and it might not al-

I n today's postmodern world, the relational bridge might be the *only* way you can reach certain people.

ways be the best way. However, in today's postmodern world, the relational bridge might be the *only* way you can reach certain people.

It's hard to find Christians who don't believe in evangelism, but it's easy to find people who don't do it. Your checkbook, calendar, and daily planner show what you actually value, far beyond what you say.

My friend, Warren Bird, has lived on the same street for almost fifteen years. It's a thirteen-house cul-de-sac in a suburb of New York City. It's full of young families and retirees, and everyone looks out for each other, from helping out during emergencies to picking up the mail when someone is out of town.

Through barbecues and holiday parties, the Birds have tried hard to get to know their neighbors. Warren and Michelle have also been intentional about exposing their neighbors to evangelistic events, including vacation Bible school, various small-group Bible studies, and Billy Graham's area crusades. Most of their neighbors peg the Birds not only as nice people, but also as religious and spiritual—even if the neighbors don't show much interest in conversations about God's role in their own lives. That has been somewhat perplexing to Warren and Michelle, even though they thoroughly enjoy chatting with their neighbors.

One evening in May 2000, Warren's street experienced some of its greatest activity in a decade. A family noticed smoke coming from an electrical plug in their little-used den. They called the fire department and asked the dispatcher to send someone over to check it out. Within minutes, three fully equipped fire engines rumbled down the street, accompanied by a police car (in case there was a traffic jam among the thirteen households). The flashing lights lit up the night sky as if it were daylight.

Several neighbors rushed outside to watch heavy-suited, helmeted firefighters trot into the house. One firefighter carried an axe. Another wore an air tank on his back.

It was quite a show. Eventually the police officer told the neighbors that everything was fine, no fire had erupted, and the fire engines would be clearing out soon.

The next morning Warren saw one of the family members as she was walking her dog. "Are you folks OK?" he asked.

Looking Warren in the eye, she pointed her finger at him and said with a smile, "You were praying for us!" The woman went on to explain all the unusual circumstances that had led the family to discover the smoking plug in a room they rarely entered, the minimal damage that had occurred, and the fact that, since it was new wiring and was still under warranty, it wouldn't cost them a penny to replace.

Warren was silent because he had not prayed about their potential house fire. In all the hoopla of wanting to help the night before, he hadn't done the most basic and important task of all: to call on the Lord. "I felt so terrible," Warren said as we talked about it later that week. "Here was my open door to put feet to my faith, and I blew it."

I disagreed. I told Warren this was really a victory. It wasn't about his failure in that one instance. He had indeed prayed for his neighbors on many other occasions.

The neighbor saw Warren as a person of genuine spiritual influence. In the crisis, the neighbor saw God—and Warren was linked to God! In fact, Warren was God's arms wrapped around that family. What more could Warren have wanted? The moment cashed in on all the tiny and big ways he had shown love to this family—from basic friendliness to inviting various family members to spiritual events such as the neighborhood men's Bible discussion groups that Warren had launched over the years.

> Credibility comes from the power of relationships. That's what trust can do.

The story gets better. The longer Warren is in the neighborhood, the more credibility he finds he has with various neighbors. Credibility comes from the power of relationships. That's what trust can do.

When the Birds were new to the neighborhood, Warren didn't have the clout to look his most spiritually resistant neighbor in the eye and say what he voiced to him recently: "Harry, I know you're not into this God stuff, but you've got to deal with it sometime. So why not do so when you're surrounded by your friends here in the neighborhood?" Out of his friendship with Warren and the other neighbors, the man showed up for a men's group that focused on Jesus' parable of the prodigal son (from Luke 15). He didn't say much and he didn't come back, but that was the most personal, spiritual discussion he'd ever been a part of with Warren. And Warren is convinced that their conversations will continue.

KEEP THE FOCUS ON A RELATIONSHIP WITH CHRIST

Being "religious" is not the same as being "alive in Christ." According to researchers Richard Cimino and Don Lattin, "You hear it everywhere from spiritual seekers and true believers, five words that are rapidly becoming the mantra of the new millennium: 'I'm into spirituality, not religion.'" They affirm that "in the post-denomination era of religion, spirituality and experience edge out doctrine and dogma."[6]

"The mantra of the new millennium [is]: 'I'm into spirituality, not religion.'"—Richard Cimino and Don Lattin

The younger the person is, the stronger these feelings are. George Gallup, Jr., gives the results of a study showing that "Most young Americans believe it is 'very important' that life be meaningful and have a purpose. Yet a high percentage of these same people believe that 'most churches and synagogues today are not effective in helping people find meaning in life.'"[7]

Many people today also look at organized religion with great skepticism. Evangelist Luis Palau once told his audience that he wasn't sure Christianity was relevant, but he was absolutely convinced that Jesus Christ was extremely relevant to society. His statement resonated with today's anti-institutional attitudes. Then, having won the audience's curiosity, Palau elaborated on how the teachings of Jesus Christ influence sociology, psychology, economics, family stability, politics, and the call of eternity.

The best way to get around people's false stereotypes of Christianity is to build a personal trust, show by your example what it means to be "alive in Christ" (see Romans 6:11; Ephesians 2:4-5; Colossians 2:13), and keep your focus on the person's relationship with God.

If your faith has become dull, irrelevant, and lifeless, the only known "cure" is to give away as much as you have to as many people as possible. We regain our "first love" for God by returning to the experiences that first kindled that love (see Revelation 2:4-5).

To get around people's false stereotypes of Christianity, build a personal trust and show by your example what it means to be "alive in Christ."

BE WHAT YOU SEEK TO CREATE

I was sitting on a couch in the Atlanta airport one afternoon, reading a newspaper and waiting for my flight. Two guys who were carrying clipboards sat down next to me.

"Uh, excuse me, sir, but, umm, do you mind if we ask you a couple of questions? You see we're taking a survey."

"OK," I said, expecting a sales pitch of some sort.

"Uh, ahem, OK. First question. Well, uh, are you traveling today, sir?"

Folding my newspaper, I looked at the guy in disbelief and answered, "Well yes, Einstein, I am!"

"Uh, OK, OK, then, umm, what airline did you come in on?"

"United."

"OK, what airline are you flying out on?"

"United."

"OK, if you were to die today and God asked you, 'Why should I let you in to my heaven?' what would you say?"

I whispered, "Wait a minute, are you trying to evangelize me?"

That spooked my questioner. He didn't expect me to know his tribal language.

"Uh, umm, yes," he timidly replied.

"Well, praise God!" I bellowed.

Heads turned all over the concourse.

"Shhhh!" my new friends the evangelists hissed as they tried to silence me. "You mean you're a Christian?" one of them asked me.

"Yes," I whispered.

"Whew!" they exclaimed. Without saying it, they indicated immense relief at not having to talk to someone who was not already a follower of Jesus. Their tenseness evaporated and they became eager to chat. They would have stayed with me all afternoon if they could have.

Something was very wrong with that picture. To me, that experience typified at least four problems with evangelism today.

First, these two Christians weren't really there to take a survey. They were proselytizing. Why do we think we have to lie to someone in order to share the greatest story ever told? What harm does it do to our message if people think we've been deceitful with them? In 1 Peter 2:1, believers are told to "rid yourselves of...all deceit." According to Revelation 21:27, deceitful people cannot enter heaven. The hearts of these two men were no doubt in the right place, but why did they undercut their credibility when they didn't need to?

Second, what message did their body language communicate? They were clearly uncomfortable. They wanted God to use their boldness, but they seemed tremendously relieved that I wasn't just another happy pagan. Their well-intentioned but anxious manner spoke far louder than their words.

Expert speech communication theorist Albert Mehrabian has shown that, in a face-to-face setting,

- 55 percent of the meaning is communicated by the body,
- 38 percent by the tone of voice, and
- only 7 percent by the actual spoken words.[8]

These statistics illustrate what any good communicator already knows: "If a speaker's verbal and nonverbal communications contradict each other, it is the nonverbal that will be believed."[9] Or as communications expert Suzette Haden Elgin says, "When the words and the body language don't match, believe the body."[10]

When I ask churches or conference groups, "What images come to mind when you think of the word 'evangelism'?" the feelings that surface are usually the fear-filled stuff associated with a cold-turkey, SWAT-team style evangelism. If my methodology makes me afraid to tell others the greatest news of my entire life, then I need to find a better method.

Third, I have every confidence that God, at times, has used people who pass out literature or knock on the doors of complete strangers. Both Warren and I have used those tactics in times past, often thinking that they were our only options in spreading God's good news. Yet most of us know that these strategies are among the very least effective ways to influence someone for Christ.

Most evangelistic programs are impersonal, but most evangelism is relational, especially today. To prove this yourself, take an informal poll in any churched setting: "How many of you came to Christ through the influence of a complete and total stranger—someone you had never met before?" I've conducted this survey a hundred times, and a very small percentage of people raise their hands.

> Most evangelistic programs are impersonal, but most evangelism is relational.

Next change the question to "How many of you became a Christian through the influence of a relative, friend, associate, or neighbor?" Typically 60 percent to 95 percent of the people raise their hands.

Finally, ask yourself the question—Did *you* respond to Christ because of the influence of a total stranger? My guess it was because of a relative, friend, associate, or neighbor.

If you've ever participated in a door-knocking method of outreach, I know what you were probably praying as you walked up to the door. Most people are hoping that no one will be home! If so, is it any wonder why Christians are not winning the evangelism game?

Why do we pray that people won't be home to answer? We fear rejection, humiliation, and the unknown. By contrast, selfless living among people we know produces the greatest influence for Christ.

> Selfless living among people we know produces the greatest influence for Christ.

TRY THE "I CAN" APPROACH

Imagine specific friends coming into relationship with Christ,

Commit to finding needs you can meet,

Assume responsibility for creatively exposing them to other followers of Jesus,

Never quit praying and initiating.

RENT THIS MOVIE

Mr. Holland's Opus
(Drama, PG)

In 1965, composer/musician Glenn Holland takes a job as a high school music teacher to get his finances in order so he can return to writing the symphony he has dreamed of. At first he hates the new job, and the students show no interest in music. After thirty years of teaching, he finally finishes his opus. More important, though, he finally realizes what a powerful impact his life has had on so many people.

What to look for: What did Mr. Holland learn about the power of relationships? Recalling the section in which his opus was finally performed, talk about the specific changes that occurred in people's lives because of him. Think of his way of teaching music as an allegory of teaching the gospel. How did his teaching method change over time? How would Mr. Holland's impact have been different if he'd never changed from his original "programmatic" style?

CONNECTIONS

Evaluate your role in evangelism based on the vision of this chapter.

1. Who influenced the most important steps of your faith journey? Place a mark somewhere on this spectrum:

←most influenced by strangers   most influenced by people I knew→

2. When you have shared your faith with others, in what kind of context has it typically been? Indicate your experience on this spectrum:

←with strangers   with acquaintances→

3. If you could choose between an afternoon of knocking on the doors of total strangers or an afternoon cultivating your acquaintance with a friend who is not yet a Christian, which would you choose? Mark your choice on this spectrum.

←afternoon with strangers   afternoon with acquaintances→

4. Consult your calendar or daily planner. How many unchurched people did you meet with in the last week in a relationship-building context?

0   1   2   3   4   5   6   7   8 or more

5. How many would you like to be meeting with?

0   1   2   3   4   5   6   7   8 or more

6. What other positive statements does your calendar indicate about your potential as a relationship-based evangelist?

7. What would you like it to reveal?

8. (If applicable.) For those of you in church leadership, what do your board meeting minutes or staff meeting minutes say about the role of relational evangelism in your church's priorities?

Discussion Questions

1. Describe one of your best experiences at sharing your faith with someone else. In what ways was it relational? How was it programmatic?

2. How have you changed over the years in the ways you share your faith with others? Why have you changed in those ways?

3. What idea or line in this chapter registered particularly well with you? Why? Which idea was most unsettling? Why?

4. What will you do differently because of reading this chapter?

CHALLENGES

CHAPTER 8

PRAY AS YOU'VE NEVER PRAYED BEFORE

You must pray as if your friends' lives depend on it if you want to co-operate with what God wants to do.

BIG IDEA

I n *The Sixth Sense*, a young boy, Cole Sear, is haunted by a dark secret: he is visited by ghosts. Cole seems to have no friends, and he spends most of his time in a local church sanctuary or in a tent at home that's filled with protective religious figures. Confused by his paranormal powers, he's too afraid to tell anyone except child psychologist Dr. Malcolm Crowe.

Before Cole reveals his secret, he looks at Dr. Crowe for a long time. Then he whispers, "I want to tell you my secret now."

Malcolm blinks very slowly and says, "OK."

Cole pauses, and Malcolm waits silently. Then Cole whispers, "I see dead people. Some of them scare me."

"In your dreams?" asks Malcolm

Cole shakes his head, "No."

"When you're awake?"

Cole nods, "Yes."

"Dead people, like in graves and coffins?" asks Malcolm.

"No, walking around, like regular people," replies Cole. "They can't see each other. Some of them don't know they're dead."

Later in the movie, Malcolm and Cole are in a church sanctuary. Malcolm wonders what the ghosts might need. "What do those ghosts want when they talk to you?" he asks Cole.

Cole stops and looks over the balcony railing at Malcolm. "Just help," he replies.

"Yes! I think that's right," says Malcolm. "I think they all want that."

So Malcolm suggests what Cole might do. "You need to help them. Each one of them. Everyone wants to be heard. Everyone."

This movie offers a powerful reminder for Christians: We, too, must realize that people are already in their eternal state if they don't know Christ. Like the people in Cole's world, they're dead and they don't even know it.

> **People are dead and they don't even know it.**

Hell begins with separation from God eternally. People you know are separated from God—many are already living in private hells. In spiritual terms, people are dying, having never lived.

For all the help Cole offered, the ghosts weren't really any better off. For us, however, the story can end differently. In this world, your help can influence someone for eternity, as well as make this world a far better place.

This final section of *Lost in America* is called "Challenges" because it's up to Christians and churches to pray, love, and take bold initiative. To be successful, we must each draw on our spiritual resources of prayer, the power of the Holy Spirit, the spiritual gifts God has given us, and the

> **The starting point was, is, and always will be prayer.**

community of faith God has surrounded us with. The starting point was, is, and always will be prayer.

THE LINE IS LONG AND THE LABORERS ARE FEW

Question: What line is fifty thousand miles long, reaches around the world two times, and grows a half mile longer each day?

Answer: The line of people in the United States who are currently untouched by your church and mine.[1]

For the majority of us, a lost person is just someone somewhere else that somebody ought to do something about. In your mind right now, imagine a line of people that stretches down your street, around the corner, down the freeway, across your state, across the entire country, and circles the world at least twice (and more times if you live farther away from the equator).

The need is so huge that we can begin to understand that Jesus' first command is not that we pray for the harvest of people who need to know God's love, but for more laborers to go out, each of whom can pull a few people from the line.

What are you going to do? Just stand there? No! Pray. And then go!

PRAYER CHANGES THINGS

Michael Slaughter, lead pastor at Ginghamsburg, a United Methodist church just north of Dayton, Ohio, made a commitment on August 17, 1994, to get up every morning an hour early to meditate and pray. "I realized that renewal and revolution is based on prayer," he says. To-day, among the longtime members at Ginghamsburg, no one would say that the "before" congregation had a greater impact than the "after" congregation. But all would affirm that prayer makes a huge difference.

Washington, D.C., once known as the murder capital of the country, has experienced a dramatic drop in the crime rate during six years of sustained prayer. Intercessors for America (IFA) says the halving of the crime rate from 1993 to 1999 coincides with concerted intercession by Christians across the country and around the world. Violent crime is down 60 percent in the area, with the number of murders dropping from 454 in 1993 to 232 last year. Burglaries declined almost 70 percent, and rapes fell by 40 percent. The overall reduction was almost three times the national percentage drop. The prayer effort began in 1990, says IFA.[2]

Several towns in Texas are setting the pace nationally for praying and partnering together in evangelism. Mission Houston, directed by Jim Herrington, is typical of this movement. Its goal is to serve the body of Christ by mobilizing the whole church in the greater Houston area to take the whole gospel to the whole city and transform the city.[3]

Pray! magazine, launched in 1997, is devoted to encouraging a passion for prayer. The most amazing thing, though, is not the magazine's news reports and meaty articles, but its growth to a respectable circulation level. People from Maine to Hawaii are paying subscription fees for something that will train them in more effective prayer.[4]

The 1990s will go down in history as the most innovative decade in history for world evangelization prayer initiatives, according to C. Peter Wagner, director of the United Prayer Track and one of the co-founders of the World Prayer Center in Colorado Springs, Colorado. The ten most significant events, he says, include the first international March for Jesus, the monthlong Praying Through the Window focus on the least evangelized parts of the world, the Reconciliation Walk that retraced the steps of the medieval crusaders and included apologies to Muslims, and the publication of prayer profiles of the almost 1,800 largest unreached groups in the so-called 10/40 Window.[5]

GENUINE RESULTS COME ONLY FROM DIVINE INITIATIVE

Personal prayer is probably the most important universal practice behind life changes. If you don't pray personally, your heart becomes so empty that you die. More important, Jesus said that if you handle the private prayer task well, the fruit will be seen in public. "When you pray, go into your room, close the door, and pray to your Father, who is unseen. Then your Father, who sees what is done in secret, will reward you" (Matthew 6:6).

On the last page of my Bible is a first-name compendium of my prayer

If you don't pray personally, your heart becomes so empty that you die.

concerns, and my daily discipline is to pray this list. The list goes back for years. It covers adversaries I've faced, massive crises, and missionaries on the front lines. To the best of my knowledge, half of the people named aren't Christians…yet.

The half-hour drive to the airport is my most special prayer time. It's not just suiting up before the big game. Rather it's realizing afresh the part God plays and asking how I can cooperate with him.

We can't help people without prayer. Talking to God about his concern for your neighbors is some-thing you can do both as an individual and as a con-

We can't help people without prayer.

gregational leader. It's the starting point for answering the "now what?" questions you may be thinking about at this point in *Lost in America*.

We're privileged to be a part of God's team to accomplish his mission to others. Just as we wouldn't do anything new without first seeking guidance and encouragement from our team leader, we don't want to try to reach people for Christ without consulting God.

The power of prayer is really the power of God realized through prayer. Through prayer, "everyone who calls on the name of the Lord will be saved," as the early church proclaimed in the first recorded sermon (Acts 2:21).

These kinds of prayers are close to the heart of God. Most Christians accept the "theology of the cross" idea of sacrifice and humility found throughout the New Testament in verses such as Matthew 16:24: "Then Jesus said to his disciples, 'If anyone would come after me, he must deny himself and take up his cross and follow me.' " Other key references are Romans 8:17 and Philippians 2:5-8 and 3:10.

Yet we regularly neglect an important part of that theology. We overlook Jesus' mission—the reason he was there on the cross, says Kent Hunter in *Move Your Church to Action*. "A theology of the cross is incomplete without the mission," Hunter says. "When Jesus calls us to take up our cross and follow him (Matthew 16:24), he is also saying, 'Take on that passion for those who are lost.' "[6] The mission aspect of the cross is to reach all people so that they will openly proclaim that

Jesus Christ is Lord, according to Philippians 2:9-11: "Therefore God exalted him to the highest place and gave him the name that is above every name, that at the name of Jesus every knee should bow, in heaven and on earth and under the earth, and every tongue confess that Jesus Christ is Lord, to the glory of God the Father."

WHY THE NEED TO PRAY IS URGENT

This past weekend, up to 75 percent of Americans did not find their way to a house of worship. If surveyed, these three out of four of our neighbors would identify more with the spirituality of Ted Turner, Oprah Winfrey, and Deepak Chopra than with what the Bible teaches us about Jesus.

What are these modern-day prophets teaching? In August 2000, media mogul Ted Turner gave the keynote speech to the Millennium World Peace Summit, a United Nations conference that gathered one thousand swamis, ministers, monks, and other spiritual leaders from around the world.

Turner, the founder of CNN, was honorary chairman of the peace summit. He played a key role in bringing it about, and he helped sponsor it financially. He told how his boyhood dream of becoming a missionary was soured by religious intolerance. "I was going to be a man of the cloth...I was going to be a missionary," he said.[7] But Turner explained that he turned away from the church because he found that it was "intolerant because it taught we were the only ones going to heaven."[8]

According to many at the Millennium World Peace Summit, the so-called intolerance of Christians only incites hatred and suppresses religious freedom. A Buddhist master received a standing ovation when he condemned all attempts at religious conversion, something at the heart of Islam and Christianity. "We have to marginalize religious leaders who are peace spoilers and are inciting hatred," said Rabbi Arthur Schneier, in an apparent reference to Christians.[9] "Let us put an end—an immediate end—to strife in the name of religion," Wande Abimbola, a Yoruba priest said, in reference to Christian missionaries.[10]

Christians are certainly to pray for peace and be agents of peace (see Matthew 5:9; Romans 14:17; 1 Peter 3:11), especially in helping people find "the good news of peace through Jesus Christ" (Acts 10:36; see also Ephesians 2:14-15). The balancing line, impossible without prayer, is to be known for our love, compassion, and good deeds while at the same time representing a Jesus so unique that he could say, "No

one comes to the Father except through me" (John 14:6). It was on behalf of this same Jesus that the early church proclaimed, "Salvation is
found in no one else, for there is no other name under heaven given to
men by which we must be saved" (Acts 4:12).

Only the God who answers prayers can soften hearts and open
minds to the point that people will see the church as a connection with
an experience of God rather than as a prison for the spirit, a self-serving
social organization, or a political supporter of the status quo.

Church Discovers the Power of Prayer in Softening Hearts

Perimeter Church, located in a suburb of Atlanta, Georgia, needed
more room for growth. After many prayerful discussions, leaders agreed
that their location was not ideal for future expansion, so they compiled
a list of criteria for the new property and began the relocation search.

As they prayed and looked, they found a piece of land that met all
of the criteria on their list, but the land was zoned for a multiuse development, had interested buyers, and was priced at far more money
than the church could ever hope to raise. As the church continued to
pray, they sensed God's leading to pursue that location. The pastor
asked the church's land team to visit the seller. The seller laughed them
out of the office saying, "I'll never sell it to you for that price—and besides I probably have more solid buyers."

As the congregation prayed more, the pastor asked the team to return to the seller. Again they were rejected. After searching further and
continuing to pray, the pastor asked the team to return one more time
and promised that this would be the last time. The seller verbally accepted the church's offer. The next day a commercial buyer put down
earnest money on the same property, but the seller honored his verbal
promise to the church.

Soon after that, but before the church had obtained the use permit
from the county, the senior pastor, Randy Pope, was walking the property, praying that the congregation would have an increased community
impact on this ideally situated new location. A neighbor introduced herself and inquired what he was doing. When he told her, the woman
said, "You'll never place a church building here." When Pope asked her

why, she assured him that another neighbor, a highly placed woman who headed the homeowners' association, had opposed every other project proposed for the site. The woman added, "No one opposes her and wins."

Pope told his relocation director to meet this neighbor and become very good friends—quickly! But before he could call, she contacted him and invited him to attend the homeowners' association meeting that very night. When he asked her why she wanted him there, she replied, "I think a lot of people will be glad to hear what your church is planning."

"So you're in favor of what we are doing?" he responded, surprised.

She explained, "Jesus Christ changed my life seven years ago. At that time, God gave me a ministry of prayer and a gift of faith, and I've used this property as my prayer garden through the years. I've been asking God to use this land for his glory. Until now, I did not feel that any other potential venture would glorify God."

Today, Perimeter Church has an inviting, beautiful facility on that site. Pope adds, "Whenever we do what we think to be the will of God and do it with a heart to glorify God, we may well fail, but if we fail, we're better off. That's why we're a praying church."

IN NIGERIA, FOUR MILLION PEOPLE ATTEND A PRAYER MEETING

The largest prayer meeting in history took place on December 18, 1998. Over four million Christians attended a prayer night in Lagos, Nigeria. They prayed for young people, the government, churches, families, the nation's security, Israel, and people who do not yet know Jesus. Pastor Adeboye of Redeemed Church of God initiated the meeting. In 1997, five hundred thousand people attended a similar meeting. The church expects up to twenty million people to attend in the year 2000.[11]

PRAYERS THAT GO BEYOND "LORD, SAVE THE WORLD. AMEN"

You can pray with an unshakable level of confidence by talking to God about matters that you know are the will of God. "This is the confidence we have in approaching God: that if we ask anything according to his will, he hears us. And if we know that he hears us—whatever we ask—we know that we have what we asked of him" (1 John 5:14-15).

You can pray far beyond "Lord, save the world. Amen." You can personalize the following "always" prayers and pray to God, believing that these prayers represent God's plan for this world he loved so much that he sent Jesus to die for us (see John 3:16-18).

1. Pray for anything that is between you and God which would prevent him from hearing your prayer. "If I had cherished sin in my heart, the Lord would not have listened" (Psalm 66:18); "Humble yourselves, therefore, under God's mighty hand, that he may lift you up in due time. Cast all your anxiety on him because he cares for you" (1 Peter 5:6-7). Wrong relationship and lack of forgiveness can hinder prayer (see 1 Peter 3:1-7; Matthew 5:23-24; Matthew 6:12, 15); so can bad or evil motives (see 1 Peter 3:12 and James 4:3).

2. Pray that your life will be characterized by good deeds that are a blessing to others and that will point people to God. "For we are God's workmanship, created in Christ Jesus to do good works, which God prepared in advance for us to do" (Ephesians 2:10); "In the same way, let your light shine before men, that they may see your good deeds and praise your Father in heaven" (Matthew 5:16).

3. Pray that God will renew and build his church. "Will you not revive us again, that your people may rejoice in you?" (Psalm 85:6); "I will build my church, and the gates of Hades will not overcome it" (Matthew 16:18).

4. Pray that injustice, oppression, and corruption will end, as part of the new era that Jesus has ushered in. "The Spirit of the Lord is on me, because he has anointed me to preach good news to the poor. He has sent me to proclaim freedom for the prisoners and recovery of sight for the blind, to release the oppressed, to proclaim the year of the Lord's favor" (Luke 4:18-19).

5. Pray for the rulers of your land, as the Apostle Paul directs: "I urge, then, first of all, that requests, prayers, intercession, and thanks-giving be made for everyone—for kings and all those in authority, that we may live peaceful and quiet lives in all godliness and holiness. This is good and pleases God our Savior, who wants all men to be saved and to come to a knowledge of the truth" (1 Timothy 2:1-4).

6. Pray that people who are thirsty will find God's soul-quenching refreshment. "Jesus stood and said in a loud voice, 'If anyone is thirsty, let him come to me and drink. Whoever believes in me, as the Scripture has said, streams of living water will flow from within him' " (John 7:37-38).

7. Pray for your relatives and friends to come into relationship with Jesus, who died on the cross as a ransom for all. "For there is one God and one mediator between God and men, the man Christ Jesus, who gave himself as a ransom for all men—the testimony given in its proper time" (1 Timothy 2:5-6).

8. Pray that God will open doors of divine opportunity for you to share the good news of life change through Jesus Christ. "Devote yourselves to prayer, being watchful and thankful. And pray for us, too, that God may open a door for our message, so that we may proclaim the mystery of Christ, for which I am in chains" (Colossians 4:2-3).

9. Pray that God will grant much fruitfulness as you invite others to follow Jesus Christ. "Finally, brothers, pray for us that the message of the Lord may spread rapidly and be honored, just as it was with you" (2 Thessalonians 3:1).

10. Pray for the restraint and defeat of Satan. "Your enemy the devil prowls around like a roaring lion looking for someone to devour. Resist him, standing firm in the faith, because you know that your brothers throughout the world are undergoing the same kind of sufferings" (1 Peter 5:8-9).

11. Pray for additional workers to help people who are spiritually receptive. "Then he said to his disciples, 'The harvest is plentiful but the workers are few. Ask the Lord of the harvest, therefore, to send out workers into his harvest field' " (Matthew 9:37-38).

12. Pray that your church will be the kind of sending church that is constantly reaching out to others. "How, then, can they call on the one they have not believed in? And how can they believe in the one of whom they have not heard? And how can they hear without someone preaching to them? And how can they preach unless they are sent? As it is written, 'How beautiful are the feet of those who bring good news!' " (Romans 10:14-15).

PRAY ABOUT THESE WRONGS, DIFFICULTIES, AND STEREOTYPES

People both in and outside of the church have many disappointments about God; many of these you can pray about, helping people overcome their concerns. Frank Harber points to the following ten objections that people sometimes raise. Whose name comes to mind for prayer as you imagine someone voicing the following objections and doubts?

1. What about the Christian I know who is a hypocrite?

2. Haven't Christians committed atrocities against others?   *(continued)*

3. Isn't Christianity a crutch?

4. Isn't it a pretty limited view to think that Jesus is the only way to God?

5. Isn't truly being a good person all that matters?

6. What about all the people who have never heard about Jesus?

7. Isn't the Bible filled with errors? How can it be "the word of truth"?

8. Why is there evil if God is loving and good?

9. Why is there so much pain and suffering in the world?

10. Why would a loving God send people to hell? [12]

THE IRONIES OF PRAYER

Hospital waiting rooms are terrible places to work on a book. The background noise and interruptions are constant, even in the critical-care waiting area. I was there prayerfully waiting while doctors removed what we thought might be cancer from my wife Jodi.

The guy sitting across from me saw me deep in concentration on the book and asked, "What are you doing?"

"Working," I said impersonally.

"On what?" he asked, unfazed.

"This is really not a good time," I said to myself. Then I said to him a bit curtly, "I'm writing a book."

"Wow! What about?"

"It's complicated," I responded, stalling, not wanting to be rude.

"Great," he replied. "I'm an engineer. I love complicated things."

"I can't win," I thought to myself. Then I said to him, "Well if you're an engineer you probably understand deadlines, because I'm facing one. I have to get this done today."

"Sure, sorry. I'll let you work," he said. "I guess I'm just a bit nervous."

"Now what am I going to do?" I asked myself. I laid down my pen.

"Really, what about?" I inquired, this time with sincere interest.

"It's my son's surgery."

"My wife's in surgery right now too. What's up with your son?" I asked.

"He's twenty-eight months old. We learned that he has Down syndrome. They're lengthening his esophagus today. On top of that, my wife left me a few months ago. She abandoned the family and is gone."

For whatever reason, right or wrong, this man's life had come undone, and he was on his own today.

"I just don't feel like I have any hope in this world," he confided in me.

I sensed he wanted some kind of response. He watched me put my work project back in my briefcase. Then I slid one seat closer.

"I'm Tom. What's your name?"

He told me his name and a bit of his background. He had gone to a Christian-sponsored boarding school as a child, but had never found a spiritual center for his life.

"What's your wife in surgery for?" he asked.

I explained our sudden cancer scare of recent days.

"You seem pretty calm about it."

I explained that a long time ago, someone had led both Jodi and me to a life of hope and showed us how to hope even in life's harshest moments.

"What do you mean?" he asked.

I cut to the chase: "The Jesus of the Bible, who I follow each day. I came to the point of admitting that I couldn't run my own life, and I realized that he could. He wanted to give me a clean heart, a clear conscience, and purpose in life, too. From there he led me to a lot of people, called a church, who come together around that same kind of discovery."

I told him about all the expressions of concern Jodi and I had experienced that morning—phone calls, e-mails, and even offers to come with us to the hospital. I concluded by saying, "Without this strong center that comes from Jesus Christ—who is every bit as real as you and me—and the changes he made in my life, the community of people he placed us in, I don't know how I'd make it.

"Wow," he said. "I wish I had that, too."

"You can," I replied.

"What do you mean?" he asked.

Over the next ten minutes, even with all kinds of noises and people around us, he prayed with me, telling God that he was sorry and receiving Jesus Christ as his Savior.

We exchanged e-mail addresses. His son's surgeon appeared, so he shook my hand and apologized that he had to go.

I sat there alone, inventorying my agenda, my initial frustration at the interruption, and the contents of this book that you're reading. I thought, "God in your mercy, you chose this moment to remind me of what's really most important."

I again surrendered myself to God to be used by him.

As if to confirm that God had heard me, the people sitting a few chairs down—who had watched my previous conversation and prayer—came up to me and asked, "Would you pray with us, too?" They had seen the other man floating in the ocean, hanging on to a life preserver, and asking for help. They, too, wanted prayer for their loved ones in crisis.

For the rest of that morning, I felt a little like I was in Africa again giving away food and water in Jesus' name. When Jodi came out of surgery, I told her what had happened. Without pausing for a nanosecond she said, "Well, then, that's why we were here today." She continues to believe that this was the reason we went through the trial.

No Bypass to the Role of Prayer

If Jesus Christ is God, then there is no sacrifice too great to make for him.

The world-renowned football coach, Vince Lombardi, walked into a football locker room and said, "Gentlemen, this is a football." This oft-repeated dictum, known by most athletes, reinforces that champions and championships are built on the basics. For the Christian, there's no substitute for a life of talking to God in prayer, and then learning to listen and find his reply.

In 1997, the Florida Marlins won the World Series, but the next year they came in last with 108 losses—the worst record in the league! Why? The year the Marlins won the World Series, the team worked out together during the off-season, kept an eye on each other's extracurricular activities, and treated each practice like a pennant game. But during the following year, management traded or sold off some of the best players, and the players were distracted with photo opportunities, promotional activities, endorsement contracts, and they focused on everything except baseball. The priority had shifted from championship performance to capital profitability, from baseball to business; and while the financial statement may have shown a profit, the fans were disappointed, disillusioned, and disgusted.

In short, everyone lost. The team not only lost games, but people also lost their passion for the sport. For the Christian, like the athlete, the main thing is to keep the main thing *as* the main thing.

"Being confident of this, that he who began a good work in you will carry it on to completion until the day of Christ Jesus" (Philippians 1:6). God wants to use you, too, "for it is God who works in you to will and to act according to his good purpose" (Philippians 2:13).

Too often in American culture, prayer has been our last resort rather than our first response. Prayer is the fuel of supernatural living. Prayer isn't a program to be added, so much as a power to be released if churches are to reach their highest potential. Prayer is your most vital tool in God's service. Pray as if your friends' lives depended on it.

> Too often in American culture, prayer has been our last resort rather than our first response.

If you have no workable prayer pattern already, would you commit to the following very practical strategy—inspired by Dr. Alvin Vander Griend, executive director, Houses of Prayer Everywhere (HOPE). He teaches people a five-and-five prayer challenge. "The idea is to pray five blessings on five neighbors starting at five minutes a day, five days a week, for five weeks. One person who accepted the challenge was a pastor in Walnut Creek, California, named Johnny Jones...Jones reported that within a month, one neighbor came to the pastor and said, 'I've always wondered what it means to have a personal relationship with Jesus Christ.' Jones saw her come to faith in Christ. Another neighbor came to Johnny, admitting an involvement in drugs and asking for help. A Buddhist Vietnamese neighbor asked to go to church with him. A Roman Catholic couple asked him to start a Bible study." [13]

Prayer unleashes the awesome firepower of the limitless resources of heaven's unstoppable forces. This energy can't be measured in megatons, kilowatts, or horsepower. It can't be stopped, squelched, or slowed. It can't be deterred, detoured, or delayed. When submitting to the will of an all-powerful, all-merciful, and all-knowing God, Christians position themselves in the place of victory prior to the commencement of the battle. Without prayer, the Christian chooses to fight a foe of unimaginable power with nothing but good sentiments, and he's doomed before the engagement begins. As prayer authority E.M. Bounds, a lawyer turned minister, has said, "Prayer is not preparation for the battle. Prayer is the battle!"

MOVING YOUR PRAYER LIFE FROM "BUSY" TO "ACTIVE"

Does it sometimes seem as if you're too busy even to pray? We're not supposed to be so busy that we're overwhelmed according to Robert Wicks, author of *Living Simply in an Anxious World*.

You can shift your life from "busy" to "active." Here's how:

1. "Never say you are busy…This will serve to stop reinforcement of the busy image; no longer will you get reinforced to be a martyr. Give up the overworked, underappreciated image.

2. Say no to people's request for your time…[or] give an enthusiastic maybe and tell them you will get back to them tomorrow. This will give you 24 hours to decide what you really want to do, to structure your response, and…to set limits for your time and energy.

3. Be present to the now. No matter how active you are, you always can deal with what each day presents if you don't preoccupy yourself with the rest of the demands facing you.

4. The choice is yours. Prayerfully allocate your time each day so that you're available to what God has in store for you." [14]

RENT THIS MOVIE

On the Waterfront
(Crime/Drama, Not Rated)

Adapted from a Pulitzer prize-winning exposé, this 1950s movie tells the story of the penetration of a longshoremen's union in New York by organized crime. One of the workers, Terry Malloy, unintentionally serves as an accomplice to murder for the evil union boss. Terry then struggles with his conscience. Meanwhile a priest named Father Barry gets involved, calling for the workers to stand up to the intimidation and evil around them.

What to look for: We're not told about Father Barry's prayer life, but imagine that everything good that happened came as an answer to prayer. What turning point in the story was the greatest answer to prayer? How did Father Barry "reach" Terry? How did Father Barry gain the longshoremen's confidence, convincing them to break the code of silence? What did you like about his cargo-hold sermon, and why?

CONNECTIONS

Praying Specifically for People to Become Followers of Christ

1. Pray specifically for one or more lost people to come to a faith relationship with Christ through the ministry of your church. Be as specific as you can in your prayer, claiming the following Scripture:

"The Lord is not slow in keeping his promise, as some understand slowness. He is patient with you, not wanting anyone to perish, but everyone to come to repentance" (2 Peter 3:9).

2. In prayer, offer yourself to be God's instrument to the person you just prayed for, as one hungry person telling another hungry person where to find an unending abundance of food. Tell God that if you can find the opportunity, you will initiate a conversation about spiritual matters.

3. Discuss some of the most effective spiritual conversation-starters you've heard or experienced, and consider which ones might work best for you.

Discussion Questions

1. What's been the greatest answered prayer you've ever experienced?

2. What's something new you learned about prayer today?

3. Pray for one of your friends who needs the love of Christ. Write down a specific verse you can claim, which you read in this chapter or knew beforehand.

4. On a scale of 1 (low) to 10 (high), how would you rate your prayer life? How satisfied are you at that level? If you'd like to change, what's one step you will take today?

CHAPTER 9
LOVE AS YOU'VE NEVER LOVED BEFORE

Here's what your church can do to enter its finest hour of relationships.

BIG IDEA

The touching movie *Simon Birch* portrays the childhood years of a boy who's extremely small for his age. He's the smallest baby ever born in his town, and he's still a foot or two shorter than his schoolmates. Despite his many physical limitations, he has an unwavering belief that God made him that way because of a special, heroic plan in store for him.

Simon also can be quite a troublemaker. One December, after he throws the church's Christmas pageant rehearsal into total chaos, he's sent into the pastor's study for a talk with the Rev. Russell.

Simon decides to use this counseling moment as a way to learn more about the divine plan in his life. "Does God have a plan for us?" he asks.

"I like to think he does," the pastor replies.

"Me, too. I think God made me the way I am for a reason," Simon says. "I think I'm God's instrument—that he's going to use me to carry out his plan."

Russell has a less optimistic view of Simon. "It's wonderful to have faith, Simon, but let's not overdo it," he replies.

Simon leaves the office to rejoin the rehearsal. After Simon is gone, Russell says sarcastically to himself, "God's instrument!"

By the end of the movie, Simon's premonitions prove to be true. When a school bus accident throws him and his classmates into a freezing river, Simon realizes that this is the moment for which he was made to be God's instrument. Buoyed up by his faith in this distinctive divine calling, he repeatedly puts his life at risk and saves the entire busload of children by crawling through a window that only someone of his tiny size could fit through.

RELATIONSHIPS THAT COUNT

Like Simon Birch, when churches and individuals give themselves wholly to Jesus' mission of the cross, they take on more influence than they ever dreamed. To follow Jesus is to be marked by God, bearing the supernatural fruit of "love, joy, peace, patience, kindness, goodness, faithfulness, gentleness, and self-control. Against such things there is no law. Those who belong to Christ Jesus have crucified the sinful nature with its passions and desires" (Galatians 5:22-24).

> **When churches and individuals give themselves wholly to Jesus' mission of the cross, they take on more influence than they ever dreamed.**

When God is their director and purpose-giver, Christians find life's ultimate relational fulfillment as they follow Jesus' calling to seek and save lost people. This pathway inevitably leads a church to enter its finest hour of relationships, hallmarked by God's kind of love.

By contrast, why do Christians so often lose their influence on others? Talk to anyone who waits on tables and you'll hear that we've lost the capacity to love.

One of the best teachers of this truth is a waitress at the Happy Chef restaurant in Huron, South Dakota. Her teaching began about 2 a.m. My colleague and I opened the door and could see that we were the only customers. We observed the cook cleaning the stove and the waitress working on a crossword puzzle.

Noticing us, she came over. "They run you boys out of the bar?" she asked in a chatty, friendly manner. Without asking, she gave us coffee and continued to make us feel welcome.

My friend smiled a bit uncomfortably and indicated that we hadn't been to a bar.

"Then what are you doing out so late?" she asked.

"Well, ma'am we're ministers," my friend replied, offering our names.

The waitress's demeanor immediately changed. "Oh," she said acidly and walked away. The room became ice-cold. We looked at the menu and waited for her to take our order. She didn't even look at us.

Soon I couldn't stand it, so I walked over to her. "Excuse me," I said. She looked up.

"I'm sorry. I don't know what happened to you from a minister or a church, but I'd like to apologize for all of us." I was doing my best to come across as well-meaning.

She blinked once and said dryly, "Whatever."

I wanted to die. She obviously did not want to let me open the subject deeper. I asked meekly, "How about if we order something to eat?" She got her pad and followed me, and I sat down. She stared blankly at us, took the order, and wordlessly walked away.

Later when she brought the food and silently poured more coffee, I noticed two letters tattooed on her arm—they happened to be the initials of my pastor friend. Trying to break the ice I asked, "How come his initials are tattooed on your arm?"

"Oh that," she replied. "That was the biggest mistake of my life, and I'm sure you couldn't care less." (Actually she used stronger language.)

Whatever she was going through was now breaking my heart. I got up. "Nobody's here. Why don't you come sit down?" I asked. "We'll double whatever you make an hour in our tip," I offered.

She came over and sat down.

"What happened?" we asked.

She unpacked a heartbreaking story of a church leader who had made unfounded promises about helping her. She became teary-eyed. "I can't talk about it," she said and went into the kitchen.

She came back a while later. "Know what?" she queried. "Do you know what you people do?" She pulled out a blow-up plastic dachshund. The words emblazoned on one side, "I love Jesus," had been changed to something blasphemous.

"This is in the kitchen," she said. "One of you people left that as a tip. How am I supposed to feed my baby with it?"

The silence that followed was awkward. Both my friend and I could think of times when we had lived down to her caricature of restaurant customers who are cheap, rude, demanding, and gossipy.

If she had commented further, I could imagine her saying with sarcasm, "Gee, I want to give my life to Jesus so I can become like that?"

I could imagine her saying with sarcasm, "Gee, I want to give my life to Jesus so I can become like that?"

We thanked her for her honesty and for teaching us about our own faith. We shelled out a very generous tip and left. She needed a community marked by integrity and genuine love. Instead, she experienced a community that had let her down hard.

If you think this story is uncharacteristic of the reputation of Christians, consider this comment e-mailed by one of several friends who read an early manuscript of the book. "This story is so true," he commented. "I have found in my community that Christians are losing credibility more through bad business dealings and attitudes than in any other way. Our daughter has her first secular job. She's a waitress at a Tim Horton coffee and donut shop. She has been more disappointed by Christians than by non-Christians."

We're losing the game not because we've forgotten what to say, but because we've forgotten how to love. Imagine what could happen to individual Christians and their churches if all we did was love at levels that we've never loved at before.

> We're losing the game not because we've forgotten what to say, but because we've forgotten how to love.

BEST LOVE LEADS TO BEST RELATIONSHIPS

I was working with a church on the East Coast and was concerned that very few people were deciding to follow Jesus Christ. I began investigating. I decided that the first problem was with me for not being intentional enough about building caring relationships outside the church.

I began to develop some new friendships. The chief of police in our community was new in that role, and so we had one thing in common: both of us had no clue what we were doing. I asked him, "What should the church be doing in our community?" Through our discussions, we built a relationship. I developed a relationship with the local director of family welfare services, and I made friends with the administrator of the public school system. I also got to know a regular waitress at a little restaurant and coffee shop where we church folks hung out after our elder board meetings and church services.

Over time, I was able to present the idea of a relationship with Christ to these four people on different occasions. All four gave the same reply: "I don't want to become a Christian. I don't want to receive Jesus as Savior and Lord. I don't want to trust him for my salvation."

"Why not?" I asked.

What they told me was painful to hear. These are the people churches say we are in business to reach.

DUMB MAY BE A VIRTUE, BUT STUPIDITY IS A CHOICE

Either through world-class stupidity or divine inspiration, I asked these four people if they would tell the congregation why they didn't want to accept Christ. I designed a four-part sermon series that would be preached primarily by people who were self-admittedly not in the fold. I realized that this might offend some people and cross some dangerous boundaries, but I was convinced that we needed to hear these stories.

On the first Sunday, the chief of police shared the pulpit with me. He talked about the sheer terror that police officers felt when the radio crackled with the news of a domestic disturbance. They knew there was more likelihood of being hurt in a situation like that than at a bank robbery.

He told us that when he first started his career in law enforcement, he could go to a high school career day and tell students that being a police officer was a noble profession. "Today," he said, "it's more like being a human garbageman."

He looked the congregation in its collective eye. "I've been in your homes at 3 o'clock in the morning, and I've seen how you behave," he continued. "It didn't matter who was Christian or not because it seemed like we arrested as many church people as nonchurched people." After a pause, he concluded, "It seems to me that if this Jesus you believe in was really true, it would affect how you behave."

The next week, my phone rang off the wall. People were upset. But that was only Round One.

The second week, the director of child and family services offered her rationale for not receiving Christ. It was because of the pain in her past. I knew she identified herself as an extremely angry, feminist lesbian who had major complications in her life. What I did not know about her story—and learned that morning—was that she had grown up in a preacher's home. She went on to describe the distance she saw between the Jesus of the Bible and the Jesus of her church. She told of the very painful early development years of her life and the awful hypocrisy that violated her as a person.

A very deep sense of sickness descended upon our people. That concluded Round Two.

For Round Three, the school board administrator said, "I don't want to receive Christ because if this Jesus was really real in you, I believe you would be known for what you are *for*, rather than for what you are *against*." His image of a Christian was an angry person who opposed a lot of things that he supported.

The speaker in Round Four was the waitress from the coffee shop. She called me the day before and asked, "Is it OK if I bring some of the girls from the coffee shop with me?"

"You bet," I answered.

Then she asked me cautiously, "Do you think it would be OK if we sang a song before I talk?"

"What song?" I said.

"Many times before we open in the morning we like to sing the old songs like 'Amazing Grace,' " she replied.

I wish you could have heard these three women as they sang an a cappella, three-part-harmony, melt-your-heart arrangement of "Amazing Grace." Then she stood in the pulpit and said that the real reason she couldn't give her life to Christ was because of the people she had to wait on each Sunday.

She told us why she didn't like to work on Sunday, and it wasn't because it was the Lord's Day. It was because of the clientele. She said, "Church people are the most demanding, rude, insensitive, cheap, gossiping people, whose children are out of control. That's just not the kind of person I'd like to become if I joined your church." I'd heard that before, in the restaurant in South Dakota.

Week five marked the beginning of a season of cleansing and repentance in that church. I can't begin to describe it. The net result was a lot of criticism and heartache. We lost some people. But what we gained at the very bottom of the trough in the life of that church was an upswing. And a mighty season of harvest began.

At issue is not that we need to learn new words to say. It's not that we lack the means. Rather, as Paul said, "Without love, I am nothing" (see 1 Corinthians 13). Jesus modeled and taught the kind of love that gives with no expectation of return. "If you love those who love you, what credit is that to you? Even 'sinners' love those who love them. And if you do good to those who are good to you, what credit is that to you? Even 'sinners' do that. And if you lend to those from whom you expect repayment, what credit is that to you? Even 'sinners' lend to 'sinners,' expecting to be repaid in full" (Luke 6:32-34).

What does love look like in your life and church? A "gen X" church in Mesa, Arizona, called Big Fish, fully aligns itself with historic, biblical Christianity. In its list of values as a church, it chose to put the following first: "We value a firm commitment to the building of friendships rather than just being friendly." Another value of theirs is "to actively practice the 'one anothers' of the New Testament." This refers to the fifty-nine commands in the New Testament for Christians to love, encourage, accept, honor, forgive, and otherwise build each other up.[1]

The best way to cooperate with the Spirit of God is summed up in one word: love.

Christians are carriers of the greatest story ever told. We can help people encounter the greatest hope that a person can possibly have. The only obstacle that should stand in people's way is their need to respond to the cross of Christ: What does Jesus mean to them? The best way to co-operate with the Spirit of God is summed up in one word: love.

Dare to be known first and foremost for your love, and see what will happen. First Corinthians 14:1 could be paraphrased, "Make love your number one aim."

First Corinthians 14:1 could be paraphrased, "Make love your number one aim."

CLOSE & PERSONAL

Urban Congregation Learns How to Show Jesus' Love

"You're nuts," friends told Rockwell (Rock) and Karen Dillaman back in 1984. "Why would anyone resign from a thriving, growing suburban congregation like yours and move to a discouraged urban church in Pittsburgh?" Even clergy who typically championed the cause of overseas missions offered the same cautions. "Haven't you heard that the area is full of the wrong kinds of people?" they lamented.

Ignoring these well-intentioned counselors, Rock became pastor of Allegheny Center Alliance Church in Pittsburgh, Pennsylvania. The Dillamans moved to within blocks of the church, and today they proudly call the community their home. They love their neighborhood and have no desire to live anywhere else.

"If you were to sit on the front stoop of our home," Rock says, "you'd hear a couple out on their porch partying on a nightly basis into the wee hours of the morning, until someone phones 911 and the police take the drunken husband away. Three doors up to the left is an intersection where a young woman sells her body each night through prostitution. Just around that corner are two homes where people sell drugs. Sometimes they blatantly stand in the center of the street to hail the cars that drive down from the wealthy suburbs."

Allegheny Center's downtown neighborhood still has as many needs as it did in 1984, but today it's full of people who've been touched by the church. The congregation used to be an all-white, fortress-mentality group that commuted in from the suburbs and intentionally made its African-American neighbors feel unwelcome.

Today Allegheny Center, 2,500 people strong, is delightfully multi-ethnic, from staff to lay leadership, and it sponsors a host of local outreaches. Even the mayor of Pittsburgh has gone out of his way to praise the church for making a difference in the community.

These changes can be traced back to Rock's desire to preach the gospel in every sense of the word. "When I sought the Lord for what to do," explains Rock, "he gave me a simple marching order from Matthew 14:35—the description of what happened when people 'recognized Jesus.' As we act like Jesus, people will come and bring those who are broken, devastated, and in need of a healing touch from God."

The idea of striving in the Spirit to look like Jesus permeates Allegheny Center Alliance Church today. "That kind of evangelism is the clear teaching of God's Word," says Rock. "I just had to jettison lots of baggage from my Western culture and my religious tradition and take a fresh look at who Jesus is."

RENT THIS MOVIE

Dead Man Walking

(Drama, R)

A nun who befriends a convicted murderer on death row experiences powerful emotions from the victims' families and also from the accused himself. As the clock ticks toward execution day, the viewer gradually comes to know the truth about the crime that occurred. In addition to helping with practical, earthly matters, the nun also tries to serve as a guide to salvation.

What to look for: What does the nun do to enter her finest hour of relationships? What did she teach others about God through her example? What difference does she make? Talk about ways you can show that same intensity of love to people in your world who are desperate to see God's genuine love.

CONNECTIONS

It's Boneheaded When It Lacks Love

Some things people do in the name of evangelism, while meant well, are boneheaded because they lack love. Read the examples following, then try to identify two things you have done, seen, or heard about that build barriers between you and those you'd like to point toward

Christ—these are things you definitely don't recommend that others use! After each example, explain why it's boneheaded.

For example,

1. Leaving a tract instead of a tip at a restaurant.
   Why it's boneheaded: *The wait staff can't put food on the table at home with tracts.*

2. Inviting someone to a concert and hiding the fact that the announced intention is evangelistic.
   Why it's boneheaded: *It's rude, insensitive, intrusive and...well... lying!*

3. Going door to door to share the gospel, but praying that no one will be home.
   Why it's boneheaded: *If you hope they're away, then you're not going out because you love them.*

Now it's your turn to think of examples.

4. Example:

   _____

   Why it's boneheaded:

   _____

5. Example:

   _____

   Why it's boneheaded:

   _____

 ## Discussion Questions

1. Is it true that the last thing many Christians are known for is their love? If so, why? Why is it so easy to not be a loving person?

2. What would a truly loving church look like? How can Christ make a person truly loving?

3. How would you live if you were a more loving Christian?

4. What is the greatest challenge for you to be more loving?

5. What are some ways you've felt embarrassed as a Christian as you've tried to show love? What did you learn from these situations?

CHAPTER 10

GO WHERE NO ONE HAS GONE BEFORE— NEXT DOOR

If you don't have friends outside the church, there's something wrong with you—and your version of Christianity.

BIG IDEA

When we watch the movie *Crocodile Dundee*, we laugh when someone from the sparsely populated Australian outback finds himself in New York City, takes the time to introduce himself to strangers, and says, "I'll be around a couple of weeks; I'm sure we'll see each other around." It's humorous because we think, "In a community of thousands or even millions, why try?"

The irony is that it really works outside the movies. It can happen anywhere. It can happen to you. It can even happen through your church.

"Where angels fear to tread, Heartland Church has already been there." That's what one person in the community said about the congregation where my family and I have been members for the last seven years. The church utterly and entirely exists outside of itself to embrace our city of Des Moines, the nation, and the world.

On any given Thanksgiving, people from our church spend most of the weekend at the Greyhound bus station, giving away sandwiches and kind words to people who would rather be anywhere else that day than in a bus station. It's one of the most participated-in activities for our church.

At Christmas, you'll find us caroling in local bars. On Easter, we're holding our celebration at an outdoor service among the downtown poor. We start off the fall with a back-to-school bash, assisting children in downtown housing projects who wouldn't have any school supplies if it weren't for our church.

We don't wait for holidays or special events. The Des Moines Register regularly highlights the most dangerous intersections in town, and we send teams there to pray for a reduction in the number of accidents— and we can demonstrate that the accident rate has dropped after we've prayed. During times of violence between ethnic gangs, teams from our church have gone to the areas and prayed—and the violence has been reduced.

I've been involved with prison outreach, prayer teams, and ministry to the urban poor. I'm proud to be part of a church that generously supports missions, from sending missionaries to Papua New Guinea to local sponsorship of refugee families.

Steve Poetzl, pastor of Heartland Church, understands that evangelism involves a process. He has led us to become a selfless group of people whose aim is not perfection, but love.

The one danger in this kind of outreach is that it can become a "drive-by" kindness. It helps your church with *Mobilizing for Compassion* (to borrow the title from Bob Logan and Larry Short's excellent book[1]), but it doesn't necessarily lead to ongoing, peer-level relationships.

My solution has been to make it a point to find friends outside of the church through my hobbies and in my neighborhood. When we lived in Rockford, I played in the city golf league rather than in the church golf league. Here in Des Moines, we've met all kinds of parents through our children's friends in the public schools. We patronize the same businesses—gas stations, dry cleaners, restaurants, and more. The proprietor of the hardware store I frequent became a good friend who eventually became the town's mayor.

I've even made friends with the United Airlines station manager at the airport. One time an unexpected water main break caused huge traffic delays. Marti saw my name on the day's flight manifest and phoned me at home to provide a heads-up alert.

I've built all these relationships not just because I'm outgoing. When I meet Christians who say they don't have any friends outside the church, I try to ask some probing questions. I usually discover that the reason is not because they're incapable of making friends. Rather, they're misunderstanding the gospel. They're thinking like consumers— it's for *me*, to solve *my* issues, *my* problems, and *my* dysfunctions. They think the point of the gospel is individual—for *my* benefit alone.

The problem for most people is not a lack

The problem for most people is not a lack of social skills but a lack of God's perspective.

of social skills but a lack of God's perspective. If we don't have friends outside the church there's something wrong with us—and our version of Christianity.

BUILDING A BRIDGE FROM ONE SIDE IS POSSIBLE!

Reaching out to your friends may feel as if you're building the world's most challenging bridge. But as the following illustration demonstrates, it can be done—even if you have to build the bridge from one side only.

The 469-mile Blue Ridge Parkway, consistently ranked as America's most scenic drive, almost didn't happen. The controversy surrounding a crucial 7½-mile segment stalled construction for twenty years. At issue: How to build a road at an elevation of 4,100 feet while minimizing environmental damage?

PHOTOGRAPHY © HUGH MORTON

The construction of the "missing link" which skirts Grandfather Mountain in North Carolina is nothing short of a triumph of modern engineering. It also demonstrates innovative solutions to significant environmental issues. The cornerstone of that segment is the 1,243-foot Linn Cove Viaduct. Claimed to be the most complicated concrete bridge ever built, the viaduct curves around the side of boulder-strewn Linn Cove.

The viaduct was assembled from one side, and the road itself was the only access allowed for construction. Builders constructed the viaduct from the top down to minimize the environmental impact—this eliminated the need for a "pioneer road" and heavy equipment on the ground.

The entire "missing link" was dedicated in 1987 and has been enjoyed by millions of travelers since then, with few appreciating the extraordinary measures required to build the bridge.

If anyone doubts that a bridge can be built from one side only, this section of the Blue Ridge Parkway is real-life proof. Likewise, evangelism is unilateral love. It's building a bridge from my life to someone else's, many times without any response from the other side until the bridge has been connected.[2]

Remember That Sinners Aren't the Enemy

How do you view people who aren't following God? Sinners aren't the enemy—they're prisoners of the enemy. The most hardened gangbanger or happy pagan is behind enemy lines, and too often we're merrily flying by in our helicopter without stopping to make a rescue.

When I lived in Virginia Beach, a young man from our community, on his 33rd sortie to bomb targets over Baghdad during the Persian Gulf War, was hit by anti-aircraft missiles. He parachuted into the heart of enemy territory. For three cold, miserable nights he hid. His right leg was shattered, and his heart was filled with fear. He hoped against hope that someone could get him out.

Back in our community, you've never seen such a mobilization of support, love, care, and prayer—all focused on the rescue of one individual. We knew the signal from his emergency beacon was fading with each passing day.

In the wee hours of the third night, the Navy SEALs pinpointed the young man's position and swept in with helicopters to pull him out. They rescued him and brought him back to base. The word flashed around our city that this man who we thought was dead was alive. It was a time of great celebration.

Everyone wanted to mark him as the hero, but he shrugged it off. "I'm not a hero," he said. "I'm just a guy who got in a bad way. The real heroes are the guys who got me out."

Rick Warren says, "You don't judge an army by how many people come and sit in the mess hall. Instead, the impact of an army is based on how many trained soldiers are out in the field, protecting, defending, or fighting the enemy." [3]

SPECIFIC SUGGESTIONS: GIVE ME PRACTICAL IDEAS

From Lewis and Clark's westward expedition two hundred years ago to *Star Trek's* galaxywide explorations hundreds of years in the future, our culture has given Christians an appreciation for going where no one has gone before. I'm reluctant to suggest specific pathways for you to take because I don't want to lessen the importance of seeking God or finding his unique niche for your life.

We can't become what we need to be by remaining what we are. If you want to come into renewal, hang around people who are seeing new converts. Hang out with a different crowd, a missionizing crowd. Together, meet unchurched people where they are, speak a language they can hear, tell them what Jesus has done for you, and invite them to make a similar decision—or to come somewhere with you where someone else will present the gospel.

The intent of *Lost in America* is to help you "morph." A caterpillar and a butterfly are the same creature, but in totally different forms. If I can build your awareness and illustrate it with practical examples, I'm confident God will show you the specific pathway and what must be done.

Where can your church begin to explore after making its prayerful missionary study of how to reach out in your community? Don't rest until you find God's vision for you and for your congregation as a healthy, reproducing, multiplying church, impacting every element of the society around you. Many of the ideas offered so far have targeted you individually; although there's overlap, here are ten ideas for your journey, all of which can be done through your church.

1. Pray in community regularly and by name for lost or unchurched people you personally know.

Prayer requires discipline, which doesn't come easily in American culture. That's where the body of Christ comes in. As Solomon said long ago, "Though one may be overpowered, two can defend themselves. A cord of three strands is not quickly broken" (Ecclesiastes 4:12). There's strength in numbers.

Recruit a prayer partner, add prayers for specific people to your mealtime routine, develop prayer cues (such as before you dial the phone), form or join a prayer ministry that focuses prayer on the unchurched in your community, start a prayer journal, or ask a friend to keep you accountable about prayer.

The possibilities are endless. In fact, why not pick up the phone right now to find a way to connect your prayer burdens with the prayer life of others.

2. Start or join a new small group.

Every growing church will cut itself down to a size at which it can care for its people. Relationships do not occur naturally in a church. The best way to build friendships in a church is through small groups.

> Relationships do not occur naturally in a church. The best way to build friendships in a church is through small groups.

My friend, Warren Bird, insists that he doesn't have the gift of evangelism. He has repeatedly asked God for that gift because he has such a passion for people to be reconciled with God. He keeps bumping into people hungry for God, but too often Warren can't lead them through the door to God.

More than once Warren has met incredibly open people. Recently, he sat next to a woman on an airplane who was terrified of flying. By the time their flight had taken off, he had listened to her story, prayed aloud with her for God to calm her fears, and had pointed her to some relevant Scriptures. She was amazingly receptive, but she declined his invitation to invite Christ into her life.

On a six-hour overseas flight, a man sat next to Warren and said, "I hope you're not a Christian because I'm running away from God!" Warren replied, "In fact, Jesus Christ has wonderfully changed my life, and he can do the same for you." Yet when they landed six hours later, the man was still far from the kingdom of God.

By contrast, several people have become Christians through neighborhood small-group Bible studies that Warren has started in partnership with a couple of other Christian friends. "I'm just as handicapped at home about knowing how to draw in the net," says Warren, "but the Holy Spirit seems to do something special through these relationally driven discussion groups."

Carl George, in his book *Nine Keys to Effective Small-Group Leadership,* states that "in the next twelve months, one out of every four church-related small groups across North America will win someone to faith in Christ." These groups are not necessarily focused on evangelism and can include everything from Sunday school classes to care groups. "Your group can be part of that disciple-making harvest even if you're not an evangelist," George says. "What's important is not your group's name, but that you develop caring, nurturing relationships marked by one-another ministry...In an environment like that, people are virtually 'loved' into the kingdom of God." [4]

Sometimes churches sponsor entire new networks of small groups, such as the Alpha course, to give congregations a way to structure events in order to grow relationships in small groups and share the gospel with seekers.

3. Champion a face-lift at church that will give people an excuse to invite friends.

Acclaimed church observer Lyle Schaller says that low morale is consistently a key obstacle in most churches, especially in small-attendance congregations. The vision of the church is so foggy that people don't even know what a "win" looks like if they stumble over it.

Something as simple as a fresh coat of paint, a new carpet, an updated sound system, or a ruthless spring-cleaning project—all done by the people of the church—can lead to a quick-win boost in corporate self-esteem. As a result, people will be more excited about bringing friends, and the church as a whole becomes more willing to take risks. This process helps induce the important shift from a low-expectation church to a high-expectation church.

Sometimes a sense of embarrassment about the facilities prevents a church's membership from wanting to invite their neighbors and associates. What barriers do you need to remove so that your church will help newcomers, especially those who do not seem to have a firm relationship with God, feel welcome and wanted?

4. Develop a more guest-friendly way of helping newcomers fit in.

Many churches find it helpful to give newcomers a sense that they have a sponsor—an established family that helps someone new "break in" and form new friendships. In other churches, care teams are actively on the lookout for newcomers, not to swat them with a hit-and-run greeting, but to sit with them, walk them to their car or public transportation, and drop them a personal "glad you came" note during the week. Some churches ask their members to make a commitment to always greet at least one person they don't know before chatting with friends.

People come to church for many reasons, but if they don't find a friend before too long, they usually lose interest or look for another place of worship where they fit in better. Whatever you do, create the triggers and structures you need to help newcomers become relationally connected and move from an outsider to an insider.

It usually helps to ask some painful questions at this point. Maxie Dunnam, former pastor and now president of Asbury Theological Seminary proposes asking the following questions:

- Do we really want to know these people who are all around us?
- Do we want them in our church?
- Are we willing for our church to become their church?
- Are we willing to go where they are and engage them on their turf?
- Are we willing to spend time with them—identify with them and show genuine compassion?[5]

5. Join the most outreach-effective ministry at your church that matches your spiritual gifts.

The idea here is to move with your church, not against it. What is working well? What do people support? In areas where people are coming to faith, how is God doing it? Where do you see the greatest demonstrations of divine power in your church? How can you use your spiritual gifts to build on these? Of the three needs mentioned in Chapter 3—transcendence, significance, and community—which would you most like to seek out and help meet in others?

6. Find or help create other relational and culturally relevant contexts to bring guests to.

The goal here is to engage and use the culture without knocking it or avoiding it. Many churches build on people's hobbies and interests. You might have a Motorcycle Day, for example, where bikers go riding together or help out community service groups. There are thousands of ways to help church people relationally connect with others in their surrounding community.

My friend Chuck lives in Bismark, North Dakota, and he met Harlan while fishing. They became fishing buddies and eventually shared many profoundly spiritual conversations. For two and a half years the men shared their love of trout fishing. When Harlan and his wife hit a crisis in their marriage, they were willing to come to church. On their second visit, both responded to the public invitation to become followers of Christ. Both were baptized in the months that followed.

> The key to evangelism is not learning how to win arguments with people, but learning how to love them.

The key to evangelism is not learning how to win arguments with people, but learning how to love them. People work is an eternal investment that takes time.

7. Start a new worship service.

Long-established churches consistently report renewed vision and new levels of excitement about inviting guests when they add a new worship service, especially if it's a worship style geared to a younger, more contemporary crowd. More important, your neighbors and friends report that they feel welcome and wanted when that new service is launched. Charles Arn's book, *How to Start a New Service*,[6] is the most comprehensive guide to date on how churches can reach new people by starting a new-style service. In his book, Arn explains how a prayerfully launched new service will...

- reach the unchurched,
- minister to more people,
- reach new kinds of people,
- help the parent church shift its life cycle to a healthier point,
- allow for change while retaining the familiar,
- activate inactive members, and
- help the parent congregation survive.

Other congregations, such as Princeton (New Jersey) Alliance Church, started a Saturday evening service because consultant Carl George told them, "Your parking lot and nursery are so full on Sunday mornings that you're turning away two hundred people each week without realizing it. They don't come because they think you're full." He was right.

8. Help sponsor, or actually participate in, a new church.

Start new churches that will love the unlovable, bring justice to unjust situations, and carry the good news of Jesus Christ to the poor. That's what the first church did, according to the book of Acts. Tradition has it that the apostles spread the gospel: Matthew went to Ethiopia, Andrew traveled to Scythia, and Bartholomew journeyed to India and Arabia.

The most compelling reason for starting new congregations is that they are the most effective way to reach unchurched people. While established churches can and certainly should be building bridges of communication to unbelievers, many churches will find the struggle and shift too difficult and may be unable to reach new generations for Christ. The same is true with various language groups. Thousands of new churches must be established across America if the gospel is to reach everyone. As C. Peter Wagner, an authority on church growth, explains, "The single most effective evangelistic methodology under heaven is planting new churches." [7]

Our mandate in spreading the Word is to remove barriers that inhibit people from hearing the good news and to build bridges of clear communication. Pastor and futurist Leith Anderson says, "the future belongs to those who start new churches" [8] because new congregations consistently have the privilege of experiencing the highest percentage of conversions and new growth of any other type of church.

CLOSE & PERSONAL

New Church Gives Hundreds of People a New Start

She was a 44-year-old professional woman, outwardly as successful as anyone could imagine. She had risen to the top of her company, and she earned a fat, six-figure salary. But her relational and emotional life was the pits. She had gone through two divorces and was discouraged.

Then she was invited to Faithbridge, a United Methodist church in greater Houston that, at the time, was just ten months old. She had received several mailers from the church, and she was curious about it.

She began attending, and through the New Connections membership class, she received Christ as her forgiver and leader. She made many new friends, and she eventually volunteered to take a huge pay cut so she could serve as the fast-growing church's full-time business administrator.

She sums up her story by saying, "For the first forty-two years of my life, I didn't know I was lost. For the next two years, I knew I was lost, but I couldn't figure out how to get found. Thanks to Faithbridge, God has found me now!"

This woman is typical of the people Faithbridge is reaching. "Some have a churched background," explains Ken Werlein, founding pastor. "But they had never come to an understanding of the gospel or personal faith in Jesus Christ. That's as real a problem in our area as for the people in other sections of the country who have never crossed through the door of a church."

As this woman attests, people think they've "got it" until they stumble into a community like Faithbridge and they realize they didn't have it. That's one of the reasons Faithbridge has zoomed from 87 people at its first Sunday morning worship service in December 1998 to more than 800 people within its first two years.

Werlein regularly leads the church to guard against becoming too "Christianized" and to continually reawaken its evangelistic thrust. He watches carefully to make sure the congregation doesn't shift to an inward focus. "We pray over everything from our sound equipment to our mailers," says Werlein. "Each worship service is covered by a rotating team of intercessors, and the first hour of our monthly Leadership Community is given to worship and prayer circles. We're so passionate to make a difference in our community that we tell our people, 'If you don't have friends outside the church, there's something wrong.' "

9. Revise your church budget to identify and increase spending in the specific areas related to evangelism.

Our church checkbooks and budgets say a lot about what we consider to be important. What could your church do to make a far larger financial commitment to evangelism, both locally and globally?

The starting point is to find an appropriate setting for examining the church budget section by section. Some churches have a budget committee that can do this specialized study. Or offer to help with that in your church. Other congregations would be open to a general resolution such as, "For the next budget year, this church will direct at least 5 percent of its general fund income to the evangelizing of this community, including training church people and hosting events designed to build bridges of outreach."

In many settings, money follows vision. Find and highlight the most exciting outreach successes—the areas God seems to be blessing the most. Urge decision makers to commit the funds necessary to expand those kinds of programs.

ROB THE REMAINING 94 PERCENT, BUT DON'T SACRIFICE GLOBAL FOR LOCAL

AIDS is now the number one killer in sub-Saharan Africa, and churches are increasingly involved in combating the AIDS crisis. According to World Relief president Clive Calver, AIDS is Africa's "greatest disaster" as well as "potentially the single biggest factor in the growth of the African church... As 23 million Africans face death, many are finding Jesus and seeking to use the remains of their lives for him." [9]

Lost in America applauds all efforts to address the spiritual and physical needs of people around the world in the name of Jesus. Local evangelism should never take away from a global emphasis. Nor should the two be in competition for the same slice of a church's resource pie. Instead we're urging a "both-and" strategy—reach people both locally and globally. The need is huge *everywhere*.

The average church spends about 3 percent of its budget and resources on local outreach and at best 3 percent overseas. We urge you to increase both of those amounts dramatically by whittling down the remaining 94 percent that a church typically spends on itself.

94%

6%→

10. Phase out programs or committees that make people too busy.

Unless a program or committee is building relationships, it's working against what the church is designed to be. Being busy may be a chief American virtue, but it's not necessarily a Christian virtue. The same was true in Jesus' day. There's a continual need to remember that "no one pours new wine into old wineskins. If he does, the wine will burst the skins, and both the wine and the wineskins will be ruined. No, he pours new wine into new wineskins" (Mark 2:22). If a program or ministry doesn't bear fruit, get rid of it.

HOW TO INCREASE EVANGELISM BY YOUR SMALL GROUP

1. Make reaching out to the lost your highest priority.

2. Find a "spark plug"—a person who is excited about bringing unbeliever-filled households to the Lord and to cell life, as Andrew did with Peter (John 1:41-42).

3. Pray fervently for lost people, fasting on occasion as well.

4. Develop personal relationships and show Christ's love.

5. Sow God's Word in casual and intentional conversations.

6. Plan ahead. Think about what to do when a person comes to the Lord.

7. Persist in reaching the lost. Don't give up.[10]

DON'T MOVE THE LINE!

After the tragic 1999 earthquake in northwest Turkey, many newscasts asked how towns could have been more prepared and buildings could have been more sound. The National Public Radio program *All Things Considered* gave one of the most unfortunate stories of all.

Apparently, some thirty years previously the people in one of the small towns in that region had been informed by authorities that the town was situated right on top of a major fault line. The danger was so significant that authorities suggested that the community relocate.

The citizens gathered to discuss the issue. Their response was a solemn town council vote to move the fault line on the map, rather than to move the town.

Many paid for that unfortunate decision with their lives.[11]

Likewise, many people today live on fault lines. Some of the faults are seen and some are unseen. Regularly we agree to move the line instead of moving our ministry.

We move the fault line whenever we limit our relationships to people who are already living in safety. I vote in my heart that the fault line is unimportant when I allow my friends to keep building their lives on the fault of hopelessness, fully aware that a seismic shock lies just beneath the surface and can cost them eternity. I need to deal with the fault line by building relationships.

If people are separated from us by an ocean and a different language, we tend to be more eager to spring into action. But when the people at risk are the people in my world who look like me, sound like me, and value the same kinds of things I value, I'm more reluctant to face the ugly fact that I'm building on a fault line. If I don't pray, if I don't love, and if I don't go, then I'm in utter denial of the impending shifts beneath the soil.

Is my inactivity because I refuse to believe that there's an earthquake coming? Even when all else fails, don't move the line. Instead pray, love, and go. Help make this world a better place, and help populate heaven for the next age, through one loving relationship after another.

RENT THIS MOVIE

The Straight Story
(Drama, G)

The Straight Story is based on the true experience of a man who rode a John Deere lawnmower across two states to see his distant, ailing brother. It's "a multilevel exploration of the goodness and beauty of America. At one level [it's] a slow walk through the heartland, its kind inhabitants, and amber grain; at another level [it's] about growing old and remembering what is important—and actively forgetting what isn't."[12]

What to look for: What kind of role model is set by the main character's willingness to engage all kinds of people in conversation? How did the power of love provoke him to do incredible things— to go where he hadn't dreamed of going before? How does he show his love through friendships?

CONNECTIONS

What's Your First Step?

1. If you haven't yet entered this dimension of living, begin a personal relationship with God through Jesus Christ.

2. Pray regularly and intensely for lost people you know.

3. Do fun things with them and serve them.

4. Go beyond your comfort zone by telling people what Jesus has done in your life.

5. Trust the Holy Spirit to lead you on the ultimate risk-taking journey by asking your unreached friends, "Will you turn to God through Jesus Christ and accept his loving leadership in your life?"

Discussion Questions

1. Review the main idea in the section "Remember That Sinners Aren't the Enemy" on page 135. Think of two specific harmful attitudes you might communicate to your unreached friends if you view them as the enemy.

2. How do we lessen God's importance when we adopt the following consumer mentality: "Salvation is designed primarily to solve *my* issues, *my* problems, and *my* dysfunctions—for my benefit alone"?

3. Which of the ten specific suggestions in this chapter seems best for you and your church? How will you begin?

4. What will you do next because of this chapter? When will you start?

CHAPTER 11

Is That Your FINAL ANSWER?

The only way we're guaranteed of losing our friends, neighbors, loved ones, community, and ultimately our nation, is if we fail to try to reach them—and therefore lose them forever.

BIG IDEA

I n the movie *Braveheart*, the central character, William Wallace, speaks to the army of Scotland just before the fight that history will record as the Battle of Stirling. The army of Scotland is outnumbered at least three to one. Some soldiers want to negotiate, and others want to quit. The English infantry, archers, and cavalry now appear over the hill.

A young soldier is taken aback. "So many!" he says and swallows hard.

The young man looks to a more experienced soldier, who shouts to everyone in hearing range that he's not going to stay and fight: "All right lads. I'm not dying...let's go home." The two Scots start to leave the field, and others join them.

William Wallace and his men, with faces painted for battle, arrive on the scene in time to see the exodus. The fleeing men stop and curiously watch Wallace's entrance.

After a brief greeting, Wallace speaks so that all can hear. "I am William Wallace, and I see a whole army of my countrymen here in defiance of tyranny. You have come to fight as free men, and free men you are. What would you do with that freedom? Will you fight?"

The veteran answers: "Fight against that? No, we will run, and we will live."

Wallace says in reply, "Aye, fight and you may die, run and you'll live. At least for a while. And dying in your beds many years from now, would you be willing to trade all the days from this day to that for one chance, just one chance to come back here and tell our enemies that they may take our lives, but they'll never take our freedom! *Alba gu brath!* (Scotland forever!)"

With that, the soldiers decide to fight. William Wallace had persuaded them that their lives would be misspent for anything less than a chance to set others free.

The same is true for you and me. Our spiritual freedom is misspent if we use it only for ourselves.

CLOSE&PERSONAL

Church Discovers Its "Seek Out and Welcome" Calling

In 1994, Holy Spirit Lutheran Church (ELCA) in Juno Beach, Florida, was a congregation in the midst of struggle, pain, and financial difficulties. Two years later, it had a future. The church's leadership had discovered something that brought a surge of life, enthusiasm, and joy into the congregation. "Ministries developed, new people stepped up to the plate to serve, programs were revitalized, attendance climbed dramatically, and people who disagreed with the church's direction left or took a wait-and-see perspective," recalls the pastor, Frank Wagner.

Their dramatic discovery was the simple realization of how much their unchurched neighbors mattered to God. "Suddenly, I understood that God was deeply concerned about them, that he sent Jesus Christ for them, and that he urgently wanted me and the church to do something about them and for them!" says Wagner.

It wasn't enough for the pastor to gain a renewed sense of mission. With the help of a church consultant, thirty-five active church members met for a weekend of prayer, Bible study, presentations, and group discussions. Within months, they agreed on what became their mission statement: "Holy Spirit Lutheran Church will intentionally and deliberately seek out and welcome all people—churched, unchurched, and members—and assist all in becoming fully devoted followers of Christ."

Why so many clarifiers? "I was very determined that we wouldn't merely give 'lip service' to being about outreach," says Wagner. "That's why we made sure that our mission statement clearly stated that we'd be intentionally and deliberately reaching out. These words emphasize that we have to give ongoing prayer, thought, planning, and action to make it happen."

The payoff continues to be a night-and-day contrast. The church doesn't merely claim to be a welcoming place; it truly is. "People have high expectations, and if we don't deliver clearly the wonder of God's grace, then we have nothing to offer that competes with the glitz of the world," concludes Wagner.

THE REWARDS OF THE BATTLES

Virginia Beach, Virginia, is not only one of the world's largest resort communities, but it also borders North America's largest military community. My wife and I moved into the Tidewater area just prior to the military buildup associated with the conflict in Kuwait. It was a unique experience to join a community where so many heads of households were in the armed services. When the military buildup began, people lived and breathed by the news that came from half a world away.

As Operation Desert Shield progressed, the tension began to build in our community. I will never forget the Wednesday evening when the war began, as Desert Shield became Desert Storm. The town screeched to a halt, vitally concerned about the welfare of everyone's loved ones. Families and neighbors gathered around televisions, glued to CNN's on-the-scenes coverage. It was as if the entire community was holding its breath.

People felt great pressure as they anxiously waited to learn what was happening to their loved ones. Reaching out to neighbors and friends took on a new urgency and importance.

Even more memorable than the anxieties of war were the parties that celebrated its quick end and the return of loved ones who had become heroes. One remarkable event was the salute the Navy itself gave when the troops returned. The naval air base hosted a communitywide victory celebration, rejoicing in the safe return of the troops, a job well done, and a mission accomplished. They pulled out all the stops to provide a magnificent air show, great music, tasty food, and fun children's activities.

The mood was electric. It was a celebration of life. Thousands of people who otherwise had little in common gave high fives and said thank you to each other. People realized that together we had all been a part of making history. Each of us, including civilians, had played a part.

If I've ever had a taste of heaven, that was it. As I looked across the huge crowd of military personnel—knowing that our military is said to be the most racially integrated institution in the world—I thought of God's promise that heaven will be similar, having people "from every tribe and language and people and nation" (Revelation 5:9).

Tears of appreciation streamed down my face as I heard stories of the cost people had paid in sending away their loved ones. As in my mental picture of heaven, any sense of rank seemed to have been abandoned for the day. It didn't even matter whether someone had been at home or on the front line. All anyone cared about was that each of us had played a role in doing the job together and bringing safely home as many as possible. If people had invested themselves in accomplishing the mission, then they were just as much a part of the success as the names that had made the headlines.

That was one unforgettable party! Like weddings, birthdays, first communions, graduations, anniversaries, and other milestones in life, parties like this are events we look forward to. They're times for celebration. They usually draw together a lot of joyful, happy, excited people.

An Invitation to a Better Party

The good news for Christians is that we have an invitation to an even better party. If my experience in Virginia Beach represented the festivity level for a quickly achieved military victory, then what kind of party is appropriate when someone enters eternity by beginning a personal relationship with Christ?

Does that idea somehow sound unspiritual to you? It comes from Jesus himself who says, "I tell you, there is rejoicing in the presence of the angels of God over one sinner who repents" (Luke 15:10).

Think of Jesus' words as an invitation to prepare for the biggest, pull-out-the-stops party you could ever dream of or hope to experience (see 1 Corinthians 2:9). Jesus likens the kingdom of heaven to a festive wedding banquet (Matthew 22:2) and emphasizes that he's inviting all kinds of people to it (Matthew 22:14; Luke 14:23). He said he came "to seek and to save what was lost" (Luke 19:10) and that "there will be more rejoicing in heaven over one sinner who repents than over ninety-nine righteous persons who do not need to repent" (Luke 15:7).

In some of Jesus' final words on earth, he passed that invitation, and the responsibility for inviting others, on to his followers. He said, "As the Father has sent me, I am sending you" (John 20:21).

Do you want to be part of something beyond your wildest dreams, something you could never achieve alone? All it takes is God plus available and willing people just like you. Some Christians have already discovered how to be part of that kind of party, and they're having the time of their life at it.

Your church can have more parties—the kind that even the angels in heaven throw. God wants you to believe that he could do just that in your area, with your friends, through your church, and through you specifically. You now have a pathway that can result in a lot of parties on earth and in heaven, as person after person **The first step is for you to imagine** experiences the life-changing power of **that God might want to use you, no** God's grace and is brought "home." **matter how ordinary you might feel.**

The first step is for you to imagine that God might want to use you, no matter how ordinary or unsuccessful you might feel so far, to help your friends and relatives in the community to have their lives turned right side up by Jesus Christ.

A SHORT HISTORY OF PARTIES

As history continually confirms, ordinary people linked with a supernatural God can do extraordinary things.

Look how rapidly things have changed in the last thousand years in your own region. In North America, for example, a millennium ago not one person had the opportunity to hear the Bible's descriptions of God's great love. Not one church was on this soil—or in this entire land—that could help people find forgiveness for sin or hope of eternal life through Jesus Christ. No social transformation was present by the justice, compassion, and goodwill that right-living Christians model wherever they live.

Yet someone brought the gospel to your town and to you in particular. Yes, over the years many, many horrible things have been done in the name of Christ, but a far greater number of wonderful advances have happened through people motivated by Jesus Christ. The vast majority of this continent's educational institutions were started by churches. In fact, 106 of the first 108 colleges in America were founded on the Christian faith.[1] Comparable things can be said for the impetus Christians provided for hospitals, orphanages, and retirement communities. Christians saw the needs and worked to meet them.[2]

Christians led the vanguard to end slavery, and Christians have done more to vanquish racial prejudice than any other single group. The angels have rejoiced as millions of people over the past centuries, one by one, have had a spiritual encounter with Jesus Christ and then lived transformed lives as a result.

While the media may focus on the low points of Christianity, even the most secular historians affirm that Christianity consistently leaves in its wake stronger families, better citizens, an ethic of caring, and an overall positive moral fabric. Christians attest to restored marriages, triumph over addictions, and sometimes literal, physical miracles of healing and wholeness that the medical community is unable to explain. Even medical science, which many people hold in Godlike awe, has proven that Christian virtues such as forgiveness help people live longer and happier lives.[3]

Today, God's people are still making this world a more just and compassionate place because they're motivated by a personal relationship with Jesus Christ. They may not always be noticed by the press, but "the saints among us"[4]—junior counterparts to Mother Teresa—can be found in every city and town, working in soup kitchens, in crisis pregnancy centers, and on "Habitat for Humanity"-style projects. From powerful corporate boardrooms to parent-child chats at the family dinner table, Jesus Christ influences daily decisions, values, and ethical choices across North America among the people who want to be Jesus' followers.

Through history, society has been changed by small groups of people whose convictions are downright radical when compared to the surrounding cultural norm. Jesus' followers are no exception.

THE FUTURE OF PARTIES

My friend and mentor Bob Logan writes, "Every day, more and more ordinary Christians are beginning to reach out to their communities, self-sacrificially ministering through their own hurts and woundedness or through their prophetic calling to meet people's needs and point them to Christ."[5] Does that include you?

How do you feel about *your* role in the future? "People optimistic about the future of American Christianity will plan and act on a different set of assumptions than will those who are pessimistic about the future," notes Lyle Schaller, dean of American church observers.[6]

Let's not kid ourselves: the situation is very bad. We've tried to demonstrate in *Lost in America* just how great the need is in this country. But we serve a huge God who loves to do amazing things through ordinary people just like us. We will win the war, not with swords, but

> We will win the war, not with swords, but with a towel and a basin.

with a towel and a basin—but only if we choose to fight.

When people follow Christ, God's priorities become theirs. Therefore, the choice to be involved in reaching friends and relatives is *normal* for the follower of Christ. Avoidance and disengagement are *abnormal*!

Which direction are you moving? The only real difference between cowards and heroes is the direction in which they run. Are you keeping far behind the battle lines by the way you function through your church, or are you trusting God to bring you deep into "enemy territory" where the battle for souls goes on in earnest?

It's time for a quick review of what your course of action will be. Your first step is to be more intentional about developing relationships with people who don't have a church home or a personal faith in Jesus Christ. What will you do to "give them heaven"?

I often think of a plaque I saw at the Old Seatack Coast Guard Station, which is now a museum in Virginia Beach. This building housed guards who would watch the sea, keeping track of steamers plying along this often turbulent coast. During rough weather or poor visibility, ships would strike the shoals and break up—always at times of merciless surf and currents. Without outside help, their passengers and crew would perish, crushed by the pounding surf, pulled out to sea by the heavy tides, and drowned. Their only hope was specially rigged lifeboats, known as crash boats, that the coast guardsmen would row through the furious surf. I saw sketches in which these crash boats were almost vertical as the rowers pulled on the long oars and tried to make it beyond the surf to rescue a ship's helpless crew.

Many times during rough weather I would stand on the beach watching the surf and thinking to myself, "How could anyone make it through that incredible surf? Even if it was humanly possible, how could anyone work up the courage to try?"

Then I found a small brass plaque mounted next to the exit doors near where the boats, ready at a moment's notice, rested on their perches. The plaque is hard to read because the coast guardsmen used to rub it for luck. The wording is short and to the point: "You have to go out. You don't have to come back."

> You have to go out. You don't have to come back.

What made these men go out? I'm sure their pay wasn't much. The work was grueling and the risk was high. They didn't save everyone. The decision was made long before the storms arrived. They knew that by signing up for this job, they were agreeing to go out with no guarantee of coming back.

Likewise, when Christians sign up to follow Jesus, we say we'll go out into the lives of our family, friends, associates, and neighbors. We agree that our mission is to bring back as many people as we can. If we're more concerned about the comforts of having our own needs met, then we've missed the point of our calling and of our salvation.

We don't staff the life station to earn our salvation, we staff it *because* of our salvation; not so that God will love us more, but because he already loves us; not so that he'll bless us more, but because he has redeemed us.

BIBLICAL URGENCY SAYS, "MAKE IT HAPPEN NOW"

"Behold, now is the day of salvation" (2 Corinthians 6:2, RSV).

"I must work the works of him that sent me, while it is day" (John 9:4, KJV).

"I have placed before you an open door" (Revelation 3:8).

"Open your eyes and look at the fields! They are ripe for harvest" (John 4:35).

"I am sending you" (John 20:21).

WHAT IS YOUR FINAL ANSWER?

Mrs. Lemke, my fifth-grade math teacher, took great pride in drilling multiplication and division skills into our skulls with her notorious timed tests. Long before the British hit game show *Who Wants to Be a Millionaire* spilled across the Atlantic, Mrs. Lemke had mastered the art of asking its central question, "Is that your final answer?"

In Mrs. Lemke's version, anytime two students tied for a score on a test or came up with different answers to the same question, she'd call both students to the front of the room. Then she'd ask each of us, "Is that your final answer?" Pause. Silence.

Whenever I stood up front, her question caused me to hesitate. The reply I'd been so certain about now became unclear and fuzzy. I agonized over the right response.

In recent years, the American public has loved to watch that same kind of agony on television as Regis Philbin, host of *Who Wants to Be a Millionaire*, asks people, "Is that your final answer?" Their response can lead to instant wealth.

The show is about everything our society has come to represent, reducing the American dream from decades and generations to minutes and seconds. Everything hangs on whether someone can give the right answers to fifteen questions.

Lost in America has tried to convey the same urgency in asking you, "Is that your final answer?"—but to a different question. At stake is more than whether you know your multiplication and division tables. At stake is far more than a million dollars.

> Life doesn't revolve around money, things, and adrenaline rushes. Life centers on a restored relationship with God.

Life doesn't ultimately revolve around money, things, and adrenaline rushes. Life centers on a restored relationship with God.

Lost in America has revealed the changes, choices, and challenges in a new century. First we discussed changes. The church is becoming increasingly complacent and irrelevant, and too many of our neighbors are headed toward hell as a result (Chapters 1 and 2). We then looked at our three fundamental needs: transcendence, significance, and community (Chapter 3). We also saw that the church in North America has been marginalized and that, as a result, we must learn to speak from a new vantage point in society (Chapter 4).

Second we looked at choices. Like Jesus, Christians today can walk in faith and experience the kind of compassion that compels us to care about those around us (Chapter 5). We can think and act like missionaries right in our own neighborhoods (Chapter 6). As we build Jesuslike incarnational relationships, we must avoid program-based or duty-oriented evangelism at all costs (Chapter 7).

Finally we discussed our challenges. We can cocoon ourselves, or we can put on our waders and step out to reach others. Those who are willing to take prayerful, bold, relational risks are finding God's pathway an incredible cure to their own flat, dead faith (Chapters 8-10).

The only way we're guaranteed to lose our friends, neighbors, loved ones, community, and ultimately our nation, is if we fail to try. What, then, is *your* final answer? Are you willing to give up the mediocre, ho-hum, uninspiring, run-of-the-mill, me-first, consumer-driven spiritual rut that you think meets *your* needs but that totally misses what may be a once-in-a-millennium time of spiritual receptiveness in *others*?

> What is your final answer to this time of spiritual receptiveness in others?

Will you begin an era of culturally relevant, relational, profoundly other-oriented living, far beyond anything you've ever experienced, because now you're asking God to pour himself out through you to your neighbors and friends? If so, you can look forward to a lot of joy and celebration.

THERE'S NO ALTERNATE PLAN

If you can imagine the realities of angels rejoicing in heaven, then you can also envision the following apocryphal dialogue.[7] Jesus had been crucified and resurrected, and he's just risen to heaven. Right before he left, he commissioned the disciples with the task of letting everyone know the story of his love (Matthew 28:18-20). After he disappears into the clouds, two angels remain briefly to break up the small group (see Acts 1:10).

The angels look over the ragtag band of social rejects, misfits, malcontents, and wanna-be revolutionaries who had witnessed Jesus' ascent to heaven. "If Jesus can change the world through them, then truly nothing is impossible," the angels say to each other as they, too, return to heaven.

The angelic watch commander looks up from his computer terminal as they enter. "Glory to God in the highest! Jesus did it! I've just e-mailed a news alert to all the heavenly hosts saying 'Mission accomplished.' "

"So what happens next?" the junior angel asks, joining a group of angels who are chatting with one another and reviewing the latest headlines.

A senior angel answers confidently, "Jesus trained his disciples and told them to tell others the good news. Through the way they live, and especially through how they love, others will turn to God. Those people, in turn, will make other disciples and teach them what Jesus taught. Soon enough the whole world will have the opportunity to follow Jesus and to experience his leadership in their lives."

"Wow!" exclaims the junior angel. Then, after reflecting for a minute, he continues, "But what if they blow it?"

"Jesus is counting on them," replies the senior angel. "He will soon send the Holy Spirit to empower, guide, and teach them."

"Okay, but what if they don't follow through?" the junior angel persists. "What if they get too comfortable with each other, their fame, or with their earthly possessions?"

"They have every resource under heaven to help them, from the peace of God to the power of the Holy Spirit," the senior angel replies. "When two or three Christians are together, Jesus shows up in special ways in and through them."

"Yes, but..." the junior angel continues.

Firm and resolute, the senior angel ends the discussion by saying, "There is no other plan." Letting out a long breath he explains further, "From everything we can tell, this is God's only plan. God is counting on them to make a difference."

Some two thousand years later, there is still no other plan. If it's going to be, it will happen with God at work through you and me. God's plan—nothing more, nothing less, nothing else.

From this mission, my soul can find no rest. What's your response?

HOW WILL YOU SHAPE THE FUTURE?

The world population at the time of Christ was about 300 million. One thousand years later, the world population had barely changed.

Today the population is more than six billion. Of those people, more than one and a half billion have never even heard the name of Jesus.

In the year 1000, the world's five largest cities were (in order) Cordova, Spain; Kaifeng, China; Constantinople, Turkey; Angkor, Cambodia; and Kyoto, Japan. The average Christian back then had never heard of most of these global centers, and could do little to influence them for Christ.

Today the world's five largest cities are (in order) Tokyo, Japan; Mexico City, Mexico; São Paulo, Brazil; New York City, USA; and Mumbai (Bombay), India. Chances are good that, within an hour from where you live, there are residents or university exchange students from at least one (if not all five) of those places!

In the year 1000, the largest population center north of Mexico was Cahokia, eight miles east of St. Louis, in Illinois. In A.D. 1000 its population was several thousand residents, and by A.D. 1100-1200 the population grew to 20,000 to 25,000 people. The site was abandoned by about A.D. 1400, and no one knows what became of the inhabitants. Not until 1800, when Philadelphia's population reached 30,000, would any city in the United States have more residents. Today the world's population increases enough each week to create an additional city the size of modern-day Philadelphia!

Today the largest U.S. city is New York, with more than 6 percent of the country's total population living in the metro New York area. Imagine the ripple effect if a huge movement of God took place in a major hub like New York, Los Angeles, Chicago, or Dallas-Fort Worth.

In the year 1000, the world leader in technology, industry, and commerce was China.

Today it's the United States. People have unprecedented access to every means possible for sharing and spreading the gospel.   *(continued)*

In the year 1000, the fastest-spreading faith was Islam, especially in Hindu-dominated India.

Today it's Christianity, especially evangelical and Pentecostal varieties, but not in North America as a whole. Here Islam, Buddhism, and Hinduism are all growing at a faster rate than Christianity.

In the year 1000, the greatest missionary sender was Norway, led by King Olaf Trygvesson, though often by force.

Today it's the United States, which has 23 percent of the Protestant congregations in the world and 52 percent of the world's Protestant foreign missionary force.

In the year 1000, the center of Christendom was Constantinople, Turkey.

Today it's south of the equator, either in Africa, Asia, or South America. It's clearly not in North America.[8] Imagine what our society would be like if the Holy Spirit's greatest movement began to occur here.

RENT THIS MOVIE

Quiz Show
(Drama, PG-13)

This film set in the 1950s tells the true story of a popular NBC game show. Two contestants, sealed in soundproof booths, must answer questions about various subjects. Unfortunately, the whole show is rigged: The winning contestant receives the correct answers in advance. One contestant blows the whistle, creating the biggest scandal in television history.

What to look for: The character who exposed the hoax had to make the toughest decision of his life. His agony over right and wrong portrays for the viewer the everyday dilemma of responsibility, fidelity, and integrity. Likewise, where is God challenging you and your church to do the right thing? In what ways do you have to make tough choices?

Discussion Questions

1. Which idea in this chapter was the most important to you? Which was the most unsettling? Why?

2. Describe how you became a follower of Jesus Christ. Who was most influential in your decision? How did that person influence you? In what ways can you do the same with your family or friends in the neighborhood, school, or workplace?

3. What do you want to be remembered for in this life? How can you become a more trustworthy person in the life mission or focus that you just described?

4. As you pray (Chapter 8), love (Chapter 9), and go (Chapter 10), what's your next step? If you're discussing these questions in a group, how would you like the group to pray for you right now?

APPENDIX A

HOW TO LEAD SOMEONE TO A FAITH RELATIONSHIP WITH JESUS CHRIST

GOD'S PLAN OF SALVATION

God promises forgiveness and eternal life to anyone who asks. Jesus Christ, through his death on the cross and resurrection three days later, has already paid the price for our sins.

OUR RELATIONSHIP WITH GOD

Through Sin, Humans Have Separated Themselves From God
Though we like to think of ourselves as basically good, we're deceiving ourselves if we claim we haven't sinned (Romans 3:23). Fortunately, Jesus came to help people who have sinned (Mark 2:17).

- What would you say to someone who was obviously sick but refused to go to a doctor?
- How is that like someone who sins but refuses to seek forgiveness?

The Way Back to God Is Through Jesus Christ, God's Son
A personal relationship with Jesus Christ is the only way back to God (John 14:6). Forgiveness, or salvation, cannot be earned; rather, it is a gift offered to everyone (Titus 2:11) to bridge that separation from God.

- Have you ever received a gift you didn't earn?
- Were you surprised? uncomfortable? joyful?
- Why would God offer such a wonderful gift?

To Be Forgiven, We Must Admit We're Going the Wrong Way
We must ask God to forgive our sins, and we must choose to turn to God's way (Acts 20:21).

- Do you fear that you've done something so terrible that God won't forgive you?
- What major decision has changed the way you live?
- How did that decision affect you?

Jesus Died on the Cross to Provide Salvation
Jesus' death and resurrection provided the only way to restore our relationship with

God. To receive salvation and eternal life, we must trust in Jesus' sacrifice for our sins and confess him as Lord (John 3:16; Romans 10:9).

- Have you ever trusted someone fully? Explain.
- What would it be like to know someone who loved you enough to die for you?

Salvation Through Jesus Restores Our Relationship With God

When we ask Jesus to be our personal Savior, we receive the Holy Spirit. He lives within the believer, gives power to live a Christian life (Romans 8:2, 6), and provides strength to withstand trials and temptations.

- What would it be like to have a personal relationship with God?
- What would it be like to have God's help every day?

God Has Done It All to Provide Salvation for Us

To receive eternal life, all we have to do is accept in faith what God has already done for us through Jesus (Ephesians 2:8-9).

- Would you be willing to consider accepting the salvation God is offering?
- What keeps you from making a faith commitment to Jesus right now?

SCRIPTURAL ANSWERS TO COMMON QUESTIONS

"How do I know God wants me to accept his gift of salvation?"...Luke 15:3-7

"Is salvation really a part of God's plan for my life?".....1 Thessalonians 5:9

"What does it mean to be spiritually reborn?"................John 3:1-7

"How do I know God will really forgive me?"...............Psalm 103:2-4; 1 John 1:9

"How should I ask God for forgiveness?".......................Psalm 51

"After I have accepted the gift of salvation, what kinds of things does God expect of me?"............Psalm 15; Ephesians 4:1-3

"Don't I need to straighten my life out and stop sinning before I can receive salvation?".........................Romans 5:8

Additional Scriptures

- **Salvation:** Acts 16:31; Titus 3:5-7; Hebrews 5:7-9
- **Unconditional commitment to Christ:** Luke 9:57-62
- **Belief in Christ:** John 6:28-29; 10:38; 12:44; 14:11
- **Repentance:** Acts 2:38; 3:19; 17:30; 2 Peter 3:9
- **Baptism:** Matthew 3:16; Acts 2:38; Romans 6:4; Colossians 2:11-12
- **Forgiveness:** Acts 10:43; 13:38; Ephesians 1:7
- **Holy Spirit:** John 14:26; 16:13; Acts 2:38-39; 11:15-16
- **Eternal life:** John 3:15-16, 36; 5:24; 6:40; Romans 6:23; 1 Timothy 1:16

APPENDIX B

How to Rate Your Congregation's Priority in Spreading the Good News

How to Use This Appendix

1. This self-assessment survey will pinpoint where your church is strongest, where it's weakest, and what to do next.
2. Have all the members of the pastoral staff, plus a good cross section of the church (such as newcomers and long-term members, older and younger members, men and women), fill out this survey.
3. Tally the responses and talk through the implications.
4. Plan to conduct the survey again in six months to see how you've improved.

Key

1	2	3	4
strongly disagree	disagree	agree	strongly agree

A. Worship Services That Support Evangelism *(If your church offers more than one type of worship service, choose the most evangelistic one.)*

---

1. I would feel comfortable inviting an unchurched friend to our services. 1 2 3 4
2. A newcomer would not feel embarrassed or confused about how to join in our services (when to stand or sit, where to find the readings, or what our terms mean). 1 2 3 4
3. The heart-level of congregational participation in worship would tell unchurched guests that we really believe in what we're doing. 1 2 3 4
4. Sometimes I sense that this might be the only Christian worship some people will ever attend, so they need an opportunity to learn how they can develop a relationship with Jesus Christ. 1 2 3 4
5. I worship in a way that others could describe as personally engaged in directing people toward the gospel. 1 2 3 4

Subtotal for this section (add the numbers and write the total here): _____

B. Core Values That Include Evangelism

1. Over the course of a year, there are many times in the church when people are presented with opportunities to become Christians. 1 2 3 4

2. An unbiased outside observer, looking at our church overall, would say that evangelism is important to our church. 1 2 3 4

3. At various prayer times throughout the church, we pray for spiritual progress for unchurched people we know. 1 2 3 4

4. New converts are encouraged to share their new faith with their friends and relatives. 1 2 3 4

5. I have recently evaluated the busyness in my life that prevents me from being intentional about building relationships with unchurched people. . . . 1 2 3 4

Subtotal for this section (add the numbers and write the total here): _____

C. Leadership That Emphasizes Evangelism

1. Our leaders would say evangelism is one of our top priorities. 1 2 3 4

2. Leaders at our church regularly talk about someone becoming a Christian through the church's outreach. 1 2 3 4

3. Our church leaders regularly encourage us to look for opportunities to show unchurched people the love of Christ. 1 2 3 4

4. I often hear our leaders pray that God will use this church to help people become followers of Christ. 1 2 3 4

5. Our leaders are disturbed about the "lostness" of people in our community. 1 2 3 4

Subtotal for this section (add the numbers and write the total here): _____

D. Evangelistic Training and Encouragement to Use Spiritual Gifts

1. Our church regularly offers programs or events that help Christians learn how to explain the gospel to a seeker. 1 2 3 4

2. Our church conveys the expectation that growing Christians will want to share their faith with others. 1 2 3 4

3. Christians are taught and encouraged to be intentional about spending time with friends outside the church. 1 2 3 4

4. Our church regularly emphasizes that we will be most successful for God if we use our spiritual gifts. 1 2 3 4

5. I am confident that I know my spiritual gifts and am using them.. . . 1 2 3 4

Subtotal for this section (add the numbers and write the total here): _____

E. Evangelistic Groups and Ministries

1. At least 5 percent (or more) of our church's small groups or ministries have evangelism as one of their top priorities. 1 2 3 4
2. Our leaders would be very open to a layperson starting a new outreach-focused group or ministry. 1 2 3 4
3. Many groups within our church are active in assisting people to come to know Christ. 1 2 3 4
4. Those in our church with the gift of "evangelism" have been identified and helped to find appropriate outreach ministries. 1 2 3 4
5. During the last year, I have intentionally joined or been part of a group/ministry designed to spread the gospel to others. 1 2 3 4

Subtotal for this section (add the numbers and write the total here): _____

F. Financial Support for Evangelism

1. At least 5 percent (or more) of our church budget is designed to help people find eternal life in Jesus Christ. (Examples: advertising, training events, and literature.). 1 2 3 4
2. In recent years, we have redistributed our budget to increase funding for the spread of the gospel. 1 2 3 4
3. If someone comes up with a great outreach project, the money is found or shows up to support it. 1 2 3 4
4. The way we spend our money confirms that we put priority on Jesus' Great Commission to make new disciples and bring them into fellowship and instruction. 1 2 3 4
5. I regularly look for ways to make financial investments into ministries that are involved with evangelism. 1 2 3 4

Subtotal for this section (add the numbers and write the total here): _____

Graph your subtotals here:

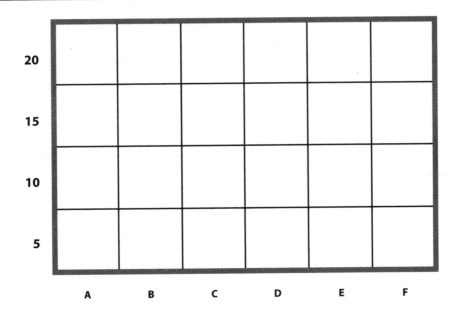

20

15

10

5

     A   B   C   D   E   F

Area of greatest evangelistic strength: _____

Area of second-greatest evangelistic strength: _____

Area of greatest evangelistic weakness:_____

Next-step action plan: _____

_____

_____

APPENDIX C

TWENTY-FIVE ALTERNATIVES FOR TELLING YOUR STORY WITHOUT CLICHÉS

HOW TO USE THIS APPENDIX

1. Find a friend who wants to learn new ways (without using clichés or the word "evangelism") to describe your faith journeys.
2. Each of you pick three of the expressions below that describe how God has worked in your life.
3. Memorize the phrases and their accompanying verses.
4. Give a short, thirty-second version and a three-minute version of your spiritual pilgrimage, using the verses and descriptions until they become comfortable and natural.

Some people, raised in churchgoing homes, affirm that they've been followers of God for as long as they can remember. Others placed their trust in Jesus Christ on a special day, such as at youth camp or when they first took Holy Communion. For yet others, spiritual growth is a long process—one they can't peg to a specific day or occasion, yet they affirm how God has at some point taken them "out of darkness into his wonderful light" (1 Peter 2:9b). The following list of expressions is designed to help you use the kind of language that others can understand as you tell your faith story.

You can describe evangelism by saying that you...

1. Learned that God leads you when you follow him.
   (Romans 8:14)

2. Responded to God's gift of forgiveness and friendship with him.
   (Ephesians 2:8-9)

3. Became an authentic and devoted follower of Jesus Christ.
   (Luke 9:23-25)

4. Quenched the emptiness you felt in your soul.
   (John 7:37-38)

5. Discovered the eternity that God makes possible through his love.
   (John 3:16-17)

6. Became a member of God's loving family.
   (Ephesians 3:14-18)

7. Found the relationship with God that you were created to enjoy.
   (Ephesians 1:4-8)

8. Entered a life-transforming relationship with Jesus Christ.
   (Acts 16:31)

9. Found forgiveness for all the wrongs you've done.
   (1 John 1:9)

10. Received Christ and became a child of God.
    (John 1:12)

11. Experienced the miracle of a new life with God.
    (John 3:3)

12. Affirmed from the heart that you want Jesus to take charge of your life.
    (Romans 10:9-10)

13. Turned away from your sins and received salvation in Jesus Christ.
    (2 Corinthians 7:10)

14. Found peace in God and became new through Jesus Christ.
    (2 Corinthians 5:17-18)

15. Met Jesus as the only entryway to heaven.
    (John 10:9; 14:6)

16. Accepted the gift Jesus gave you when he paid for your life with his.
    (1 Timothy 2:3-6)

17. Put your trust in Jesus who made a great sacrifice on your behalf.
    (Hebrews 9:22)

18. Discovered that sense of belonging that only God can offer.
    (1 Peter 2:9-10)

19. Began life's most important relationship.
    (1 John. 4:8-10)

20. Let God transform your life of fear into a life of genuine love.
    (1 John. 4:16-18)

21. Experienced true freedom through Jesus Christ.
    (John 8:31-32)

22. Ended the separation between you and God.
    (John 14:6)

23. Experienced dramatic change by giving leadership of your life to Jesus Christ.
    (Ephesians 6:7-8)

24. Discovered what it means to be genuinely fulfilled and content.
    (John 10:10)

25. Appointed Jesus as the "managing partner" or "chief operating officer" of your life.
    (James 4:7)

Additional ideas:

Accepted Christ's leadership and forgiveness.

Stepped across the line of faith toward Christ.

Discovered a relationship in this life with your Creator.

Escaped the human condition and found freedom in Christ.

Other: _____

_____

Other: _____

_____

APPENDIX D

ADDITIONAL RESOURCES

Select Tom Clegg Resources:

Releasing Your Church's Potential, Robert E. Logan and Thomas T. Clegg (Guidebook/Cassette Album), Carol Stream, IL: ChurchSmart Resources, 1998.

Seven Habits of a Visitor-Friendly Church, Thomas T. Clegg (Workbook/Audio Album), Lynchburg, VA: Church Growth Seminars, 1999.

Select Warren Bird Titles:

The Coming Church Revolution: Empowering Leaders for the Future, Carl F. George with Warren Bird, Grand Rapids, MI: Fleming H. Revell Company, 1994.

How to Break Growth Barriers: Capturing Overlooked Opportunities for Church Growth, Carl F. George with Warren Bird, Grand Rapids, MI: Baker Books, 1993.

Into the Future: Turning Today's Church Trends into Tomorrow's Opportunities, Elmer L. Towns and Warren Bird, Grand Rapids, MI: Fleming H. Revell, 2000.

Nine Keys to Effective Small-Group Leadership, Carl F. George with Warren Bird, Mansfield, PA: Kingdom Publishing, 1997.

Real Followers: Beyond Virtual Christianity, Michael Slaughter with Warren Bird, Nashville, TN: Abundant Life & Company Publications, 1999.

General:

Becoming a Contagious Christian, Bill Hybels and Mark Mittelberg, Grand Rapids, MI: Zondervan Publishing House, 1994.

Building a Contagious Church: Revolutionizing the Way We View and Do Evangelism, Mark Mittelberg with Bill Hybels, Grand Rapids, MI: Zondervan Publishing House, 2000.

The Church Between Gospel and Culture: The Emerging Mission in North America, eds. George R. Hunsberger and Craig Van Gelder, Grand Rapids, MI: Wm. B. Eerdmans Publishing Co., 1996.

Church for the Unchurched, George G. Hunter III, Nashville, TN: Abingdon Press, 1996.

Church Next: Quantum Changes in How We Do Ministry, Eddie Gibbs, Downers Grove, IL: InterVarsity Press, 2000.

Deep Change: Discovering the Leader Within, Robert E. Quinn, San Francisco, CA: Jossey-Bass, 1996.

The Gospel in a Pluralist Society, Lesslie Newbigin, Grand Rapids, MI: Wm. B. Eerdmans Publishing Co., 1990.

The Missional Church: A Vision for the Sending of the Church in North America, eds. Darrell L. Guder and Lois Barrett, Grand Rapids, MI: Wm. B. Eerdmans Publishing Co., 1998.

Paradigm Shift in the Church: How Natural Church Development Can Transform Theological Thinking, Christian Schwarz, Carol Stream, IL: ChurchSmart Resources, 1999.

A Primer on Postmodernism, Stanley J. Grenz, Grand Rapids, MI: Wm. B. Eerdmans Publishing Co., 1996.

Resident Aliens: Life in the Christian Colony, Stanley Hauerwas and William H. Willimon, Nashville, TN: Abingdon Press, 1989.

When Nations Die, Jim Nelson Black, Wheaton, IL: Tyndale House Publishers, 1994.

The following are from the *Christian Mission and Modern Culture* series edited by Alan Neely, H. Wayne Pipkin, and Wilbert R. Shenk:

The End of Christendom and the Future of Christianity, Douglas John Hall, Harrisburg, PA: Trinity Press International, 1997.

The Mission of Theology and Theology as Mission, J. Andrew Kirk, Harrisburg, PA: Trinity Press International, 1996.

The Missionary Congregation, Leadership and Liminality, Alan J. Roxburgh, Harrisburg, PA: Trinity Press International, 1997.

Secularization and Mission: A Theological Essay, Bert Hoedemaker, Harrisburg, PA: Trinity Press International, 1998.

ENDNOTES

Introduction

1. The analogy of the trees and wind came from our friend, Len Sweet, in a personal conversation.

2. This alliteration was inspired by Tom Clegg's good friend and partner in ministry, Steve Ogne.

3. Robert D. Putnam, "Bowling Alone: America's Declining Social Capital," Journal of Democracy (vol. 6, no. 1, January 1995). The text is available from http://muse.jhu.edu/journals.

4. The Newsweek poll conducted by Princeton Survey Research Associates, December 10-12, 1998, asked, "How important is it to you that non-Christians convert to Christianity? Is this very important, somewhat important, not too important, or not at all important?" Among Christians, 43 percent said "very important" and 20 percent said "important." For results, see www.polling report.com/religion.htm.

Section One: Changes

CHAPTER 1

1. The Des Moines Register and Tribune (April 13, 1970).

2. For more information, see the National Aeronautics and Space Administration's report, "Detailed Chronology of Events Surrounding the Apollo 13 Accident" at www.hq.nasa.gov/office/pao/History/Timeline/apollo13chron.html. And see the HBO documentary "From the Earth to the Moon: Part 8, We Interrupt This Program" (1998), written by Peter Osterlund and Amy Baker, directed by David Frankel.

3. From Apollo 13 (1995), screenplay by William Broyles, Jr., and Al Reinhart, directed by Ron Howard.

4. See Apollo 13 (1995), directed by Ron Howard. See also Gene Kranz, Failure Is Not an Option: Mission Control From Mercury to Apollo 13 and Beyond (New York, NY: Simon & Schuster, 2000), 306-339.

5. The sources used for these statistics include: Births (3,941,553/year), deaths (2,337,256/year), marriages (2,244,000/year), and divorces (1,135,000/year) from 1998 figures, see www.infoplease.com/ipa/A0004929.html. Abortions (1,184,758/year) based on 1997 statistics in "Abortion Statistics, 1972-1997" at www.info please.com/ipa/A0764203.html from a report by the U.S. Centers for Disease Control and Prevention. Births to unmarried women (1,257,444/year)

are 1997 figures, see www.cdc.gov/nchs/data/t1x1797.pdf. Arrests (10,295,129/year) from 1998 figures at www.infoplease.com/ipa/A0004944.html. Drug abuse violations (1,560,000/year) from 1998 statistics at www.whitehouse.gov/fsbr/crime.html. Suicides (30,575/year) from 1998 statistics at www.cdc.gov/nchs/fastats/lcod.htm. Deaths of people with AIDS (16,432/year) from 1998 data at www.cdc.gov/hiv/stats/hasr1102/table21.htm. Alcohol-related traffic deaths (15,786/year) are 1999 numbers at www.madd.org/stats/gen99.shtml, from the National Highway Traffic Safety Administration. Teenage sex information (15-year-olds, 1,690,000/year) from 1995 data at www.cdc.gov/nchs/datawh/statab/pubd/2319_19.htm. High school dropouts (479,000/year) are 1998 numbers at www.census.gov/prod/99pubs/p20-521.pdf from Gladys M. Martinez and Andrea E. Curry, "School Enrollment—Social and Economic Characteristics of Students (Update)," a September 1999 U.S. Census Bureau report. Teenage smoking data (6,000/day) is from www.cdc.gov/tobacco/research_data/youth/initfact.htm. Food stamp recipient numbers (23,100,000/year) are 1997 figures in "Number of People Receiving AFDC/TANF or Food Stamps" at www.publicagenda.org from a report by the USDA Food and Nutrition Service. Bankruptcy figures (1,239,493 non-business filings from the last half of 1999 and the first half of 2000) are based on statistics from the American Bankruptcy Institute at www.abiworld.org. (Data retrieved from Web sites on November 17, 2000. Daily statistics were determined by dividing yearly statistics by 365.)

6. Muslim conversion data is from a personal conversation with Carl Ellis, president of Project Joseph, a ministry that prepares the church to reach Muslims. Mormon conversion data (318,340 convert baptisms/year) is from Deseret News 1999-2000 Church Almanac (Salt Lake City, UT: Deseret News, 1998), 111. Baptisms and memberships, representing Protestant, Catholic, and Orthodox branches, come from examining the annual reports of many denominations and from the database of U.S. churches (all branches of Christendom) reported in the Yearbook of American and Canadian Churches 2000. Church closures from Lyle Schaller, Tattered Trust: Is There Hope for Your Denomination? (Nashville, TN: Abingdon Press, 1996), 26. New church information is our best estimate, based on personal interviews with leading authorities on church planting and numerous denominational officials; we believe that 2,000 to 2,300 new churches will be launched across the United States in 2001.

7. William M. Easum, "It's Time to Tell the Truth About Christians and Our Churches," Net Results (February 2000), 22.

8. Russell Ash, *The Top 10 of Everything 2001* (New York, NY: DK Publishing, 2000), 78.

9. Russell Ash, *The Top 10 of Everything 2001*, 78.

10. Statistics from a Barna Research Group press release, "Asians and the Affluent Are Increasingly Likely to Be Born Again" (May 30, 2000), www.barna.org.

CHAPTER 2

1. David W. Henderson, *Culture Shift: Communicating God's Truth to Our Changing World* (Grand Rapids, MI: Baker Books, 1998), 20-21.

2. William J. Bennett, "Does Honor Have a Future?" The Forrestal Lecture delivered before the United States Naval Academy, November 24, 1997. For the text of the lecture, go to www.empower.org/html/pubs/speeches/navy.htm.

3. Kent R. Hunter, *Move Your Church to Action* (Nashville, TN: Abingdon Press, 2000), 12.

4. In his book, *The Only Hope for America: The Transforming Power of the Gospel of Jesus Christ* (Wheaton, IL: Crossway Books, 1996), 48, evangelist Luis Palau writes, "Today, by George Barna's estimation based on large-scale surveys of the population, 190 million people in America have yet to trust Jesus Christ as their Savior." Researchers Win Arn and Charles Arn estimate that "there are nearly 192 million pagans or marginal Christians (Christians in name only)." In *The Master's Plan for Making Disciples*, 2nd edition (Grand Rapids, MI: Baker Books, 1998), 8.

5. Verified by personal e-mail July 10, 2000, from Eddie Gibbs, Donald A. McGavran Professor of Church Growth, School of World Mission, Fuller Theological Seminary.

6. Eileen Lindner, editor, *Yearbook of American & Canadian Churches 2000* (Nashville, TN: Abingdon Press, 2000), 10-12.

7. Population estimates from the U.S. Census Bureau at www.census.gov/population/estimates/nation/intfile2-1.txt.

8. Church attendance statistics from a Barna Research Group press release, "The State of the Church, 2000" (March 21, 2000), www.barna.org.

9. For a discussion, see Thomas C. Reeves, *The Empty Church: The Suicide of Liberal Christianity* (New York, NY: The Free Press, 1996), 62-63. And see C. Kirk Hadaway, Penny Long Marler, and Mark Chaves, "What the Polls Don't Show: A Closer Look at U.S. Church Attendance," American Sociological Review (vol. 58, no. 6, December 1993), 741-752.

10. Information from the Barna Research Group. And see the press release, "One Out of Three Adults Is Now Unchurched" (February 25, 1999), www.barna.org. But according to a press release by the Gallup News Service, "Unchurched America Has Changed Little in Twenty Years" (March 28, 2000) by Michael Lindsay, 44 percent of adults in America are unchurched, a figure that has remained relatively steady. People were considered unchurched if they answered "no" to either or both of the following questions: "Are you, yourself, a member of a church or synagogue?" and "Apart from weddings, funerals, or special holidays such as Christmas, Easter, or Yom Kippur, have you attended the church or synagogue of your choice in the past six months, or not?" Poll results are at www.gallup.com.

11. George Hunter, in a presentation entitled "The Church's Mission to Secular People" given in Chicago, Illinois, on October 17, 2000, Beeson Institute for Advanced Church Leadership.

12. Statistics from "Catch the Vision!" Mission Frontiers (November-December 1996), www.missionfrontiers.org.

13. "15,000 Become Christians Every Day in India" (April 15, 1999), in the feature story archives at www.religiontoday.com.

14. Reginald Bibby, "The Ten Key Findings," in *Transforming Our Nation: Empowering the Canadian Church for a Greater Harvest*, edited by Murray Moerman (Richmond, BC: Outreach Canada Ministries, 1998), 269-332.

15. Charles Arn, "A Response to Dr. Rainer," Journal of the American Society for Church Growth (vol. 6, 1995), 74. Warren Bird also reviewed the 1999 yearbooks from a number of denominations to confirm the ongoing validity of this claim.

16. Reginald W. Bibby and Merlin B. Brinkerhoff, "Circulation of the Saints Revisited: A Longitudinal Look at Conservative Church Growth," Journal for the Scientific Study of Religion (vol. 22, no. 3, 1983).

17. Martin Marty quoted by Jane Lampman, "New Thirst for Spirituality Being Felt Worldwide," Christian Science Monitor (November 25, 1998), 7.

18. Gerald Anderson quoted by Gustav Niebuhr, "Perceived Shift in Ecclesiastical Center of Gravity," The New York Times (May 27, 2000).

19. George Barna quoted by Andy Butcher in "'No Evidence' of Spiritual Revival, Says Report Tracking Goals and Values" (April 27, 2000), Charisma News Service archives at www.charismanews.com.

20. All quotes and data are from Dan Wooding's Strategic Times, "Awakening the Sleeping Giant" e-mail feature (January 27, 1999). The text

of this article is at www.rwcc.com/assist/code/strat025.htm. Used by permission. For more information about CHIEF, visit the organization's Web site at www.chief.org.

21. Personal communication from Thom S. Rainer. From data to be published in *The Formerly Unchurched* (Grand Rapids, MI: Zondervan Publishing House, 2001).

22. Charles Arn, "A Response to Dr. Rainer," in Journal of the American Society for Church Growth (vol. 6, 1995), 74. Arn estimates that between 3,500 and 4,000 churches close each year, and between 1,100 and 1,500 churches open their doors. Lyle Schaller, in *Tattered Trust: Is There Hope for Your Denomination?* (p. 26), predicts that 100,000 to 150,000 congregations will dissolve in the first half of the twenty-first century—an average of five to eight each day.

23. The Almanac of the Christian World, 1993-1994 edition (Wheaton, IL: Tyndale House Publishers, 1992), 485.

24. Lyle E. Schaller, *The Very Large Church* (Nashville, TN: Abingdon Press, 2000), 29.

25. Justin D. Long, "North America: Decline and Fall of World Religions, 1900-2025," from the Global Evangelization Movement's Monday Morning Reality Check (no. 5, 1998) at www.gem-werc.org. Long uses the definition of North America that covers primarily the United States, Canada, and Greenland, excluding Latin American countries.

26. Chapter in Stephen L. Carter, *The Culture of Disbelief: How American Law and Politics Trivialize Religious Devotion* (New York, NY: BasicBooks, 1993), 23-43.

27. Carl Ellis quoted by David Neff in "Answering Islam's Questions," Christianity Today (April 3, 2000), 7.

28. Wendy Murray Zoba, "Islam, USA," Christianity Today (April 3, 2000), 40.

29. Gustav Niebuhr, "The Church and the Challenge of Contemporary American Culture" in a January 8, 1999, lecture at Calvin College, www.calvin.edu/january/1999/index.htm.

30. Personal communication from Carl Ellis, president of Project Joseph. Ellis is also an adjunct faculty member at The Center for Urban Theological Studies, Philadelphia, Pa., and Columbia International University Seminary, Columbia, S.C.

31. From "The Globe at a Glance," www.missionfrontiers.org/2000/03/globeglance.htm.

32. Civilization magazine (December 1999/January 2000).

33. Justin D. Long, "North America: Decline and Fall of World Religions, 1900-2025" at www.gem-werc.org.

34. James W. Sire, *The Universe Next Door,* 3rd edition. (Downers Grove, IL: InterVarsity Press, 1997), 120-121.

35. Justin D. Long, "North America: Decline and Fall of World Religions, 1900-2025" at www.gem-werc.org.

36. Helen Rose Ebaugh and Janet Saltzman Chafetz, *Religion and the New Immigrants: Continuities and Adaptations in Immigrant Congregations* (Walnut Creek, CA: AltaMira Press, 2000), 13.

37. CNN news story, "Census Figures Show Dramatic Growth in Asian, Hispanic Populations" (August 30, 2000), www.cnn.com.

38. According to Jeffery L. Sheler in "The Mormon Moment," U.S. News & World Report (November 13, 2000), the Mormon church (the Church of Jesus Christ of Latter-day Saints) is "...one of the world's richest and fastest-growing religious movements. In the 170 years since its founding in upstate New York, the LDS church has sustained the most rapid growth rate of any new faith group in American history" (p. 59). "Nearly half of the world's 11 million Mormons live in the United States. The church's growth rate over the past 30 years far outstrips those of other major U.S. denominations" (chart, p. 61). "Church officials say more than two thirds of new members each year are converts, making the Mormon church one of the most aggressive and successful at proselytizing" (p. 62).

39. Statistics from Barna Research Group cited in Vital Ministry magazine, now Rev. magazine (July-August 1999), 19.

40. Kenneth L. Woodward, "A Lama to the Globe," Newsweek (August 16, 1999), 20-21.

41. Jody Veenker, "Paganism, Ivy League-Style" on Christianity Today's Weblog (November 8, 2000), www.christianitytoday.com. From David Abel, "Back to Nature: Paganism Growing in Popularity on Nation's Campuses," The Boston Globe (October 31, 2000), www.boston.com/globe.

42. David A. Roozen and C. Kirk Hadaway, editors, *Church and Denominational Growth* (Nashville, TN: Abingdon Press, 1993), 393-395.

43. C. Kirk Hadaway, Penny Long Marler, and Mark Chaves, "What the Polls Don't Show: A Closer Look at U.S. Church Attendance," American Sociological Review (vol. 58, no. 6, December 1993), 741-752.

44. Robert D. Putnam, *Bowling Alone: The Collapse and Revival of American Community* (New York, NY: Simon & Schuster, 2000). See also "Bowling Alone: America's Declining Social Capital," Journal of Democracy (vol. 6, no. 1,

January 1995).

45. Roger Finke and Rodney Stark, *The Churching of America: 1776-1990: Winners and Losers in Our Religious Economy,* (New Brunswick, NJ: Rutgers University Press, 1992), 15-16.

RELIGIOUS ADHERENCE

Year	% Who Claim Membership
1776	17%
1860	37%
1890	45%
1926	56%
1980	62%

46. George Gallup, Jr., "Easter Draws Americans Back to Church" (April 2, 1999), www.gallup.com.

47. See Chapter 9, "Religion," in Robert N. Bellah, Richard Madsen, William M. Sullivan, Ann Swidler, and Steven M. Tipton, *Habits of the Heart* (Berkeley, CA: University of California Press, 1985).

48. From an address by George Gallup, Jr., at the annual meeting of the Academy for Evangelism in Theological Education, Princeton Theological Seminary, Princeton, New Jersey, October 7, 2000. Also see George Gallup, Jr., and Timothy Jones, *The Next American Spirituality: Finding God in the Twenty-First Century* (Colorado Springs, CO: Chariot Victor Publishing, 2000).

49. See the Barna Research Group press release, "Church Lay Leaders Are Different From Followers" (June 26, 2000), www.barna.org.

50. See the Barna Research Group press release, "Christians Are More Likely to Experience Divorce Than Non-Christians" (December 21, 1999), www.barna.org. See also Andy Butcher "Shock Study Reveals Christians More Likely to Divorce Than Non-Christians" (December 23, 1999) at the news archives, www.charisma news.com.

51. Statistics from Urie Bronfenbrenner, et al., *The State of Americans* (New York, NY: The Free Press, 1996) cited in William J. Bennett, *The Index of Leading Cultural Indicators* (New York, NY: Broadway Books, 1999), 217-218.

52. Statistics from the Alan Guttmacher Institute cited in William J. Bennett, *The Index of Leading Cultural Indicators,* 219-220.

53. Statistics from Thomas R. Eng and William T. Butler, editors, *The Hidden Epidemic* (Washington, DC: National Academy Press, 1997) cited in William J. Bennett, *The Index of Leading Cultural Indicators,* 221-222.

54. United Nations statistics cited in William J. Bennett, *The Index of Leading Cultural Indicators,* 223-224.

55. Statistics from *Monitoring the Future* (1998) cited in William J. Bennett, *The Index of Leading Cultural Indicators,* 227-228.

56. Statistics from National Criminal Justice Reference Service cited in George Thomas Kurian, editor, *The Illustrated Book of World Rankings* (Armonk, NY: M. E. Sharpe, 1997), 317.

57. U.S. child poverty rate from the *Statistical Abstract* cited in William J. Bennett, *The Index of Leading Cultural Indicators,* 225-226.

58. Nick and Leona Venditti, *Church History 2: Renewal and Expansion in the Modern Age* (Des Moines, IA: Open Bible Standard Churches, 1996), 125.

59. From a Barna Research Group press release, "Christians Embrace Technology" (June 12, 2000), www.barna.org.

60. Statistics from The 1998 Consumer Research Study on Book Purchasing, as reported in Christian Retailing (October 7, 1999), 9.

61. Christian Retailing (June 17, 2000), 33.

62. American Bible Society advertisement in the American Bible Society Record (October-November 2000), 25.

63. John and Sylvia Ronsvalle, *The State of Church Giving Through 1997* (Champaign, IL: Empty Tomb, Inc., 1999), www.emptytomb.org.

CHAPTER 3

1. Dinitia Smith, "Success of Christian Thriller Reflects Rising Interest in Religious Fiction," The New York Times (June 8, 2000). The text is available through the archives at www.nytimes.com.

2. G. Sean Fowlds, " 'Left Behind' Tour Wows San Diego," Christian Retailing (June 17, 2000), 8.

3. And see www.drlaura.com.

4. Kim Campbell, "Media Tunes in to Religion," Christian Science Monitor (May 26, 2000). See the archives at www.csmonitor.com.

5. Alan Wolfe, *One Nation, After All* (New York, NY: Penguin Books, 1998), 55.

6. According to www.movieweb.com, on June 1, 2000, the top ten films based on domestic gross ticket receipts were *Titanic, Star Wars, Star Wars: Episode I—The Phantom Menace, E.T. the Extra-Terrestrial, Jurassic Park, Forrest Gump, The Lion King, Return of the Jedi, Independence Day,* and *The Sixth Sense.*

7. Saint Augustine, "The Confessions" in *Great Books of the Western World, 18: Augustine.* Editor in chief, Robert Maynard Hutchins (Chicago, IL: Encyclopedia Britannica, Inc., 1952), 1. Language updated to the vernacular by Warren Bird.

8. Andy Butcher, "Americans Have More Spiritual Questions, but Fewer Seek Answers in Church" Charisma News Service (January 17, 2000), using

information from a survey by the University of Michigan's Institute for Social Research. See news archives at www.charismanews.com.

9. Paul Johnson, "The Real Message of the Millennium," Reader's Digest (December 1999), 66.

10. Charles Henderson, "Why Movies Matter" (April 21, 1997), www.christianity.about.com.

11. *Unreached Mega Peoples of India* was published in 1999 by India Missions Association in conjunction with the Frontier Mission Centre Research Team. The book contains profiles, photographs, maps, charts, statistics, and prayer points for each of the major unreached peoples of India. To contact India Missions Association, e-mail to imahq@vsnl.com, or write to India Missions Association, 48 First Main Road, East Shenoy Nagar, Chennai 600 030, India.

CHAPTER 4

1. Donald McGavran, *The Bridges of God* (New York, NY: Friendship Press, 1955).

2. Nick and Leona Venditti, *Church History 2: Renewal and Expansion in the Modern Age* (Des Moines, IA: Open Bible Standard Churches, 1996), 123.

3. See the FCC's official response, "Religious Broadcasting Rumor Denied," at www.fcc.gov/cib/consumerfacts/Religious.html. See also "Urban Myths Within the Christian Community" (August 4, 1999) at Focus on the Family's CitizenLink, www.family.org/cforum.

4. Eddie Gibbs, "Developing a Twenty-First Century Church With Integration and Integrity" delivered at the annual gathering of the American Society for Church Growth, November 1998, and available on audiotape from the American Society for Church Growth, (Pasadena, CA: Fuller Theological Seminary, Center for Lifelong Learning), www.fuller.edu/cll.

5. See Peter L. Berger, editor, *The Desecularization of the World: Resurgent Religion and World Politics* (Grand Rapids, MI: Wm. B. Eerdmans Publishing Co., 1999).

6. Mark Hutchinson, "It's a Small Church After All: Globalization Is Changing How Christians Do Ministry," Christianity Today (November 16, 1998). See news archives at www.christianitytoday.com.

Section Two: Choices

CHAPTER 5

1. Moody Adams, *The Titanic's Last Hero* (Columbia, SC: Midnight Call, 1998).

2. Bill Bright and John N. Damoose, *Red Sky in the Morning: How You Can Help Prevent America's Gathering Storms* (Orlando, FL: NewLife Publications, 1998), 238.

3. Ron Hutchcraft quoted in Bill Bright and John N. Damoose, *Red Sky in the Morning,* 238.

4. Reynolds Price, "Jesus of Nazareth," Time (vol. 154, no. 23, December 6, 1999). See the Time magazine archives at www.time.com.

5. J.B. Phillips, *Your God Is Too Small* (New York, NY: Macmillan Publishing Company, 1961).

6. Terry Wardle, *The Soul's Journey Into God's Embrace* (Ashland, OH: The Sandberg Leadership Center, 2000), 23.

7. Terry Wardle, *The Soul's Journey Into God's Embrace,* 26.

8. From a Barna Research Group press release, "One Out of Three Adults Is Now Unchurched" (February 25, 1999), www.barna.org.

CHAPTER 6

1. Kent R. Hunter, *Move Your Church to Action* (Nashville, TN: Abingdon Press, 2000), 12.

2. Mark Hutchinson, "It's a Small Church After All: Globalization Is Changing How Christians Do Ministry," Christianity Today (November 16, 1998).

3. Kennon Callahan, *Effective Church Leadership: Building on the Twelve Keys* (San Francisco, CA: HarperCollins Publishers, 1990), 13.

4. From Walt Kallestad, *Entertainment Evangelism: Taking the Church Public* (Nashville, TN: Abingdon Press, 1996), 1-58.

5. The Little Bo-Peep analogy comes from Eddie Gibbs, "Church Growth Viewed Through a Glass Darkly," side 2, of a tape titled "Church Growth: Then and Now" (Pasadena, CA: Fuller Theological Seminary, Center for Lifelong Learning), www.fuller.edu/cll.

6. Mike Regele with Mark Schulz, *Death of the Church* (Grand Rapids, MI: Zondervan Publishing House, 1995), 208.

7. Randy Rowland, "Engaging the Culture for Christ" in *The Pastor's Update* audiotape series (Pasadena, CA: Fuller Theological Seminary, Center for Lifelong Learning), www.fuller.edu/cll.

8. Kent R. Hunter, *Move Your Church to Action,* 12.

9. Statistics from a Barna Research Group press release "An Inside Look at Today's Churches Reveals Current Statistics on Protestant Churches" (October 30, 1997), www.barna.org.

10. Randy Rowland, "Engaging the Culture for Christ" in *The Pastor's Update* audiotape series (Pasadena, CA: Fuller Theological Seminary, Center for Lifelong Learning), www.fuller.edu/cll.

11. From Ron Crandall, *The Contagious Witness: Exploring Christian Conversion* (Nashville, TN: Abingdon Press, 1999), 151-155.

12. Rick Warren, *The Purpose-Driven Church*

(Grand Rapids, MI: Zondervan Publishing House, 1995), 39-40; and Lynne and Bill Hybels, *Rediscovering Church* (Grand Rapids, MI: Zondervan Publishing House, 1995), 57-58.

CHAPTER 7

1. C. Kirk Hadaway, "Is Evangelistic Activity Related to Church Growth?" in *Church and Denominational Growth,* edited by David A. Roozen and C. Kirk Hadaway (Nashville, TN: Abingdon Press, 1993), 169-187.

2. George Barna, *The Index of Leading Spiritual Indicators* (Dallas, TX: Word Publishing, 1996), 7.

3. Ron Crandall, *The Contagious Witness: Exploring Christian Conversion* (Nashville, TN: Abingdon Press, 1999), 8.

4. Bill Bright and John N. Damoose, *Red Sky in the Morning: How You Can Help Prevent America's Gathering Storms* (Orlando, FL: NewLife Publications, 1998), 72. According to Candice Atherton in "The Legacy of Billy Graham: Bill Bright," July 28, 2000, "Throughout its fifty-year history, Campus Crusade for Christ has shown people how to experience God's love and plan for their lives, providing worldwide evangelism exposures to 4.8 billion people since 1951. 1999 proved to be a banner year with 1.2 billion exposures to the gospel and approximately 24.1 million decisions made for Christ." The article is available at www.crosswalk.com.

5. See Ron Crandall, *The Contagious Witness: Exploring Christian Conversion.*

6. Richard Cimino and Don Lattin, "Choosing My Religion," American Demographics (April 1999), www.demographics.com.

7. Statistics from George Gallup, Jr., "The Religious Life of Young Americans," cited in Richard Cimino and Don Lattin, "Choosing My Religion," American Demographics (April 1999).

8. Albert Mehrabian, *Silent Messages* (Belmont, CA: Wadsworth Publishing Company, 1971), 43.

9. Jana Childers, *Performing the Word: Preaching as Theatre* (Nashville, TN: Abingdon Press, 1998), 57.

10. Suzette Haden Elgin, *How to Turn the Other Cheek and Still Survive in Today's World* (Nashville, TN: Thomas Nelson Publishers, 1997), 116.

Section Three: Challenges

CHAPTER 8

1. This word picture is built on the following assumptions: (a) The phrase "currently untouched" refers to unchurched people. These are defined as people who are not church members or who have not attended services in the past six months. According to a Gallup poll (see "Unchurched America Has Changed Little in Twenty Years" [March 28, 2000] at www.gallup.com), the percentage of Americans who are not church members or who have not attended regular services within the past six months is 44 percent, up from 41 percent in 1978. (b) The current U.S. population is roughly 280 million (see the population clocks at www.census.gov). Then 44 percent of that number is 123 million unchurched people in America. (c) The 3 percent change that Gallup identified over 20 years is 0.15 percent per year. Thus the growth in the unchurched population, at 0.15 percent per year, is 420,000 per year. (d) At 2 feet per person, the estimate for a line of people is 2,640 people per mile. So 123 million unchurched people divided by 2,640 people per mile is about 46,590 miles. (e) The earth is 24,902 miles at the equator, which means the line would go almost two times around the earth. (f) The 420,000 new unchurched people per year divided by 2,640 is 159 miles/year or roughly half a mile each day. *Additional confirmation:* U.S. churches are growing, but not enough to keep pace with the population, says the *Yearbook of American & Canadian Churches 2000* (Nashville, TN: Abingdon Press, 2000), 12. For a more scholarly analysis of declining church attendance, see Robert D. Putnam, *Bowling Alone: The Collapse and Revival of American Community* (New York, NY: Simon & Schuster, 2000), 65-79.

2. "Prayer Behind Dramatic Drop in Capital Crime, Say Intercessors," from an e-mail news update by Charisma News Service (vol. 2, no. 82, June 23, 2000).

3. For more information about Mission Houston, go to www.missionhouston.org.

4. For more information, go to www.gospelcom.net/navs/NP/pray.

5. "1990s Prayer Efforts Called 'Most Innovative in History,'" from an e-mail news update by Charisma News Service (vol. 2, no. 87, June 30, 2000).

6. Kent R. Hunter, *Move Your Church to Action* (Nashville, TN: Abingdon Press, 2000), 103.

7. Colum Lynch, "U.N. Summit Hears Plea for Religious Tolerance," The Washington Post (August 30, 2000), www.washingtonpost.com.

8. Austin Ruse, "Turner Attacks Christianity at U.N. 'Peace Summit'" (dated August 30, 2000, posted August 29, 2000), at www.newsmax.com.

9. Gustav Niebuhr, "Religion's Many Faces Meet in New York for Peace," The New York Times (August 31, 2000), www.nytimes.com.

10. "U.N. World Peace Summit Draws Colorful Array of Religious Leaders" (August 30, 2000), www.chicagotribune.com.

11. Redeemed Church of God, Lagos.

12. Frank Harber, "10 Objections to Christianity," Today's Christian Woman (March/April 2000) at www.christianitytoday.com. See also Frank Harber, Reasons for Believing: A Seeker's Guide to Christianity (Green Forest, AR: New Leaf Press, 1998).

13. Elmer Towns and Warren Bird, Into the Future: Turning Today's Church Trends Into Tomorrow's Opportunities (Grand Rapids, MI: Fleming H. Revell, 2000), 103.

14. "Are You Too Busy?" (April 26, 2000), from the archives at www.liveit.net/life, excerpted from Robert J. Wicks, Living Simply in an Anxious World: An Invitation to Perspective (Mahwah, NJ: Paulist Press, 1988, 1998).

CHAPTER 9

1. For one list see Carl F. George, Prepare Your Church for the Future (Grand Rapids, MI: Fleming H. Revell, 1991), 129-131.

CHAPTER 10

1. Robert E. Logan and Larry Short, Mobilizing for Compassion (Grand Rapids, MI: Fleming H. Revell, 1994).

2. Information about the Blue Ridge Parkway is available at www.blueridgeparkway.org.

3. From a lecture at a May 2000 conference hosted by Saddleback Community Church.

4. Carl F. George with Warren Bird, Nine Keys to Effective Small-Group Leadership (Mansfield, PA: Kingdom Publishing, 1997), 6.

5. From a message entitled "Vocation of Leadership," given in Houston, Texas, on February 15, 2000, Beeson Institute for Advanced Church Leadership.

6. Charles Arn, How to Start a New Service: Your Church Can Reach New People (Grand Rapids, MI: Baker Books), 1997.

7. C. Peter Wagner, Church Planting for a Greater Harvest (Ventura, CA: Regal Books, 1990), 11.

8. From a message at a Leadership Network "Gathering of Champions" conference in Dallas, Texas, January 1999.

9. "World Relief Launches Church-Based AIDS Program in Africa to Address Africa's 'Greatest Disaster' " (June 23, 2000), World Relief press release, www.worldrelief.org.

10. Adapted from Karen Hurston, "Spark Plugs, Passion, and Evangelism," Cell Group Journal (Spring 2000), 21, 32.

11. "Turkey Quake," a report by Jennifer Ludden on National Public Radio's All Things Considered program (August 26, 1999), www.npr.org.

12. Plot summary from Barton Adrian Bean IV on the Internet Movie Database, www.imdb.com.

CHAPTER 11

1. Mark A. Beliles and Stephen K. McDowell, America's Providential History (Charlottesville, VA: Providence Foundation, 1989), 109. Also see pages 102-108.

2. See Charles Colson, "Will the Church Miss the Volunteer Revolution?" Christianity Today (vol. 36, no. 3, March 9, 1992), 88.

3. See, for example, Harold Koenig, M.D., The Healing Power of Faith (New York, NY: Simon & Schuster, 1999).

4. George H. Gallup, Jr., and Timothy Jones, The Saints Among Us (Harrisburg, PA: Morehouse Publishing, 1992).

5. Robert E. Logan and Larry Short, Mobilizing for Compassion (Grand Rapids, MI: Fleming H. Revell, 1994), 13.

6. Lyle Schaller, "Pessimistic or Optimistic," Net Results (February 2000), 3.

7. Based on a story in Joseph C. Aldrich, Life-Style Evangelism, (Portland, OR: Multnomah Press, 1981, 1993), 15-16.

8. Year 1000 numbers and current are data from the following sources: Laurent Belsie, "How Many People Does It Take to Change the World?" a Christian Science Monitor special feature on the Internet at www.csmonitor.com/athousandyears; "Status of Global Mission, 2000, in Context of Twentieth and Twenty-First Centuries" at www.gem-werc.org (retrieved November 17, 2000), which estimates the unevangelized population at 1,556,100,000; "The Year 1000," a special issue of the U.S. News and World Report (August 16-23, 1999), see also www.usnews.com; The World Almanac and Book of Facts 2000 (Mahwah, NJ: Primedia Reference, Inc., 1999), 878, which estimates the population of the New York City urban area at 16,332,000 (1995); the U.S. Census Bureau, which estimates the 1995 U.S. population as 262,803,000, see www.census.gov/population/estimates/nation/intfile2-1.txt; the World Bank Group, www.worldbank.org, which provides world development information; Justin Long, "North America: Decline and Fall of World Religions, 1900-2025," from the Global Evangelization Movement's Monday Morning Reality Check (no. 5, 1998) at www.gem-werc.org; and Patrick Johnstone, Operation World: The Day-to-Day Guide to Praying for the World, 5th edition (Grand Rapids, MI: Zondervan Publishing House, 1993), 564.

Group's

R.E.A.L.
GUARANTEE

Every Group resource incorporates "R.E.A.L. Learning"—
a unique approach that results in long-term retention
and life transformation. It's learning that's:

R = Relational
Learner-to-learner talk involves everyone, enhances
understanding, and builds Christian friendships.

E = Experiential
Learning by doing and using multiple senses increases
learning and retention up to tenfold.

A = Applicable
Connecting God's Word to the learners' real world
moves learning beyond information to transformation.

L = Learner-based
Addressing how learners learn best focuses not on
how much is taught, but on what is learned.